Cycle

Kenneth L. Sturgill

Copyright 2017: Kenneth Sturgill

All rights reserved. This book is protected by the copyright laws of the United States of America. This book or parts thereof, may not be copied or reprinted in any form without express permission from the author.

Requests of the author can be made at the following email address: ksturgill@comcast.net

ISBN-13: 978-1548919504
ISBN-10: 1548919500

Publisher:
Apostle Kenneth L. Sturgill

ksturgill@comcast.net

DEDICATION

I appreciate my wife, Phyllis, for walking in unity with me to travel the world pulling down strongholds and releasing God's will. Her discernment and prophetic releases are very powerful and we make a great team. I thank her for her vision of the book cover which is beautiful and powerful. Together, we have walked through many seasons of God and have gained much understanding and insight into the patterns of God.

I thank my church family for their desire and hunger for truth. This has enabled me to share revelations from God's word without opposition.

Our intercessors are Throne Room generals of intercession. They hear God's will and do warfare to establish His word on earth and keep us covered while we are traveling the world.

I thank Karrie Powers, a young lady in our church, who had the difficult task of deciphering my scribbled notes, typing and formatting my book.

I thank Melisa Fields of Don Fields Photography for her work on my book cover. Her art work of Phyllis's vision for my cover is excellent. They do great photography work and you can contact them at Don Fields Photography in Sevierville, TN. 865-774-7610.

I thank Dr. Renfro and Sid for taking the time out of their busy schedule to write a forward for my book. Dr. Renfro is a great medical doctor and is in great demand. Sid labors tirelessly in community work. They both travel extensively doing ministry and healing services. Sid ministers in a lot of conferences. They have their own TV program(Walking in the Kingdom) that is a great help to many people.

I especially thank our praise team for releasing the sounds and words of songs of the Lord at almost every service that releases the mind of God, His instructions and inspiration for us.

CONTENTS

Ch#	Chapter Title	Pg#
1	Introduction	1
2	Definitions	3
3	History of Seasons	4
4	Spiritual Seasons	6
5	Cycles of Seasons	10
	• Cycle #1: The Law of a Season	10
	• Cycle #2: The Cycle of Spiritual Growth	12
	• Cycle #3: Initiate Change	14
	• Cycle #4: Set Time	15
	○ Principles of Set Times	15
	▪ Principle #1: Set times have Past, Present, and Future	15
	▪ Principle #2: Your Future	16
	▪ Principle #3: Affects your destiny	17
	▪ Principle #4. Being at the Right Place at the Right Time	18
	• Place a Value on Time	18

• Purchase Time	19
• Prioritize Time	20
Cycle #5: God's Purpose for Seasons	24
Cycle #6: Instant in season and out	25
Cycle #7: Evict the Devil from New Season	26
• Pattern Jesus used to Enter His New Season of Ministry	27
○ Pattern #1. Jesus left the Past Season	27
○ Pattern #2. Jesus was lead by the Holy Spirit	27
○ Pattern #3. Jesus Defeated Satan's Temptations	28
▪ Temptation #1. Satan attacks Jesus' Body	28
▪ Temptation #2. Satan attacks Jesus' Soul	29
▪ Temptation #3. Satan attacks Jesus' Spirit	29
Cycle #8: Process of Assimilation	31
• Definitions	31
• Our Responsibilities of Assimilation	31
○ Observing and Learning	31
○ Pattern of Assimilation	32
○ Opening 4 Gates	34
▪ Eye, Ear, and Touch Gates	34

		▪ Process of Mediating	34
		▪ Confession	35
		▪ Desire to activate the Seed of Life	35
	Cycle #9: Leaving and Entering		36
6	Last Season		38
	• Part 1: Vision and Dreams God Showed Me		38
	• Part 2: Releasing a new Anointing		42
	• Part 3: Example of Unity		43
	• Part 4: Unity of Spirit, Soul and Body		44
		○ All three must be in unity	44
		○ All three must be blameless or holy	45
	• Part 5: Progressive Maturity		46
	• OUR BODY		46
		○ Eye Gate (Main Entrance of Darkness to the Body	47
		○ Ear Gate	48
		○ Touch Gate	50
		○ Summary of our Body	51
	• OUR SPIRIT		53
		○ How we reach the status of "Sons of God"	53
		○ We must be spiritually Mature	56

		○ We must believe so we can become a son of God	57
		○ We cannot have a religious spirit	57
		○ We must believe in the Holy Spirit	58
		○ We cannot believe in the Wrong Doctrine	58
		○ We must Separate ourselves from the World	60
		○ We must accept Chastening from God	61
		○ We must be peacemakers	61
		• OUR SOUL	62
7	Make Life an Adventure		64
8	Conclusion		71

FORWARD

God's magnificence is recorded in all of nature, and His creation continually testifies His greatness. Millions of people in the United States, for the recent solar eclipse, took time off, planned, traveled, and turned aside from their usual daily lives to witness that incredible event. How can anyone gaze upon these celestial bodies so intimately associated with Earth, interacting with such precision to accomplish such a wonder, without realizing and acknowledging, the Creator….., you can't. All of creation exists and operates in precise timing, in seasons and cycles to perpetuate, promote and maximize life for individuals as well as others around them. Pastor Kenneth's book on Cycles of Seasons skillfully draws from the natural world to define and explain and highlight the importance of the Spiritual cycles and season of our lives. God is a God of timing, with seasons and cycles set specifically to accomplish His will. Just as we have seasons in our lives that grow us and mature us, we also have spiritual seasons that spiritually mature us individually and as a body to become the mature Bride ready for her Bridegroom. This book explains and defines these seasons, with instruction for entering new ones and exiting old ones, as well as maximizing the current season. In understanding this, God will bless our individual lives, while affecting His will in the ministry and throughout the earth.

-Thomas Renfro MD

CHAPTER 1

INTRODUCTION

The omnipotent God is the Alpha and Omega of this world and the New World to come. By His wisdom, creation was fashioned in such intricate detail that it leads no doubt it could not have happened by mere chance. Times and Seasons was a brilliant idea as part of creation to prevent the boredom of a continued routine in a familiar setting in the natural realm and in the spiritual realm. This idea keeps an exciting expectancy and hope for our future happiness and joy. Doing the same routine every day, year after year, in our living in the natural realm and the spiritual realm leads to a failed system of achieving our full potential of maturity and reaching the full stature and image of Jesus in both realms.

The bible says, first the natural and then the spiritual.

1 Corinthians 15:46
However, the spiritual is not first, but the natural, and afterward, the spiritual.

Different cycles in new seasons helps locate us and gives us a bearing of where we are within a season.

PSALM 119:59
I thought about my ways, and turned my feet toward your instructions.

The psalmist located himself on the way (path, course of life) and changed the direction of his feet to align himself to walk one with God. Let's choose to walk the rest of our journey through life walking fully in the seasons, cycles, and the principles of the Kingdom of God.

CHAPTER 2

DEFINITIONS

The Definition of Cycle

A set of events or actions that happen again and again in the same order. It is a never ending circle. A period of time. A new season has a set time by God and a set of principles that apply in each new seasons. God is a God of order in both the natural seasons and the spiritual seasons. I pray that you will apply the same principles of cycles in each new season so you can be successful in life.

The Definition of Seasons

Hebrew – appointment, appointed times, fixed time, set time.

Greek – a season, a measure of time, implies that which time gives an opportunity to do the necessity of the task at hand. A fixed definite time.

This definition declares that a season contains a provided set time as well as an action to be accomplished inside of that set time.

CHAPTER 3

HISTORY OF SEASONS

Ecclesiastes 3:1
To everything there is a season, a time for every purpose under heaven.

Genesis 1:1
In the beginning God created the heavens and the earth.

Genesis 8:22
While the earth remains, Seed Time and Harvest, Cold and Heat, Winter and Summer, and Day and Night shall not cease.

Genesis 1:14
Then God Said, "Let there be lights in the firmament of the heavens to divide the day from the night; and let them be signs and seasons, and for days and years."

Everything that exists or will ever exist has a season. Nothing exists without a season in the natural realm or the spiritual realm. This is God's plan and man cannot stop it.

Apostle Paul, in **I Corinthians 15:46**, is instructing us of the natural realm and the spiritual realm coexisting throughout history.

Seeing the natural realm first helps us to understand the spiritual realm. Also, it implies that we must act or do something in the natural realm first to produce results in the spiritual realm. This initiates a pattern or sets a precedent requiring us to do the natural things required in order to receive the benefit of the spiritual seed as: praying, reading the Bible, giving money, and living an obedient lifestyle before we will receive the spiritual blessings from God. Therefore, man has to walk through both the natural and spiritual realm of seasons as it has been throughout history where we see nothing existed without seasons.

Adam was first nothing but dust (natural realm) then God breathed into him the Ruach (breath of God, God's Spiritual Life into his spirit (spiritual realm). God created the natural seasons first as He created the Heavens and the earth. Secondly, when He created man, He created the spiritual seasons.

Aren't we glad God created a diversity of seasons to help us have the potential of a more joyful life?

CHAPTER 4

SPIRITUAL SEASONS

We take advantage of the four natural seasons of diversity of time and climate changes to enjoy the vast activities that each season provides yet, we know every little how to enjoy and fulfill the spiritual seasons of God, and all they provide, especially the **Feasts of the Lord (Leviticus Chapter: 23).**

We have knowledge that spiritual seasons exist, but do we understand the cycles, principles, or the law of seasons? You can have knowledge of a vehicle, but until you get in and operate the vehicle you will not fully understand how to reap the benefits or enjoy the ride.

Elmer Fultz, Phyllis's dad, loved to drive and go places. He enjoyed driving around the community and praying. As he got older and couldn't react quick enough, we had to take his keys. This is one of the hardest things I have ever done. He cried and didn't want to give them up, however, he realized he was no longer able to drive safely and he didn't want to harm anyone. We need to have this same attitude to enter each season of God and enjoy experiencing the fullness that God has provided.

Proverbs 4:5-7
Get wisdom! Get understanding! Do not forget nor turn away from the words of my mouth, do not forsake her, and she will preserve you. Love her and she will keep you.

Let your heart retain my words, keep my commands and live. Get wisdom! Get understanding

Wisdom is the principal thing, therefore get wisdom, and all your getting, get understanding. Exalt her, and she will promote you, she will place on your head an amount of grace, a crown of glory, she will deliver to you.

We must have knowledge, wisdom, and understanding of spiritual seasons to walk fully in the Blessings and Peace of God. Spiritual seasons will continue until the restoration of all things are achieved, then Jesus will return.

Restoration of all things creates the long term goal conclusive to a mindset favorable to a continued achievement.

Acts 3:19-21
Repent and be converted that your sins may be blotted out, so that times of refreshing may come from the presence of the Lord, and that He may send Jesus Christ, who was preached to you before, whom Heaven must receive until the time before, whom Heaven must receive until the times of restoration of all things.

The definition of converted is to turn, turn to or towards, to turn to God.

The definition of restoration is to bring back its former condition, to set in order. Two things must occur before this happens:

1. Man must be restored to the spiritual condition of Adam before Adam sinned.
2. The bride must make herself ready and prepared to meet Jesus.

When Adam sinned, man lost all of his spiritual relationship with God. Adam was to have dominion over all things and rule the earth. So, God uses spiritual seasons to restore man to his original spiritual condition and his position of authority.

Acts 3:19
We are commanded to repent and be converted (this is written in the imperative mood and is a command) from our sins so

we can experience freedom from sins and then times of refreshing can come.

The Greek word for time is Kairos which is defined as a (set time) to perform the necessity of the task at hand. This is the set time designated by God as spiritual seasons to provide times of refreshing. The definition of refreshing is recovering of breath or revival.

This is a recovering of God's breath of spiritual life He breathed into Adam.

Presence is defined as the Face of God or His presence. This is a renewing of our spirits in special spiritual seasons from God's presence. This is when we can come face to face with God and be changed from Glory to Glory. This is the time or season when our spirits grow and mature to become the Sons of God. By entering into His spiritual seasons, we can mature into the perfect and full stature of the image of Christ.

Ephesians 4:13
Till we all come to the unity of the faith and of the knowledge of the Son of God, to a perfect man, to the measure of the stature of the fullness of Christ.

This is the part of restoration that time provides to make the changes to become more like Christ. This verse must be achieved to fulfill the definition of restoration.

Acts 3:21 uses a different Greek word for times. This word is the Greek word Chronos which defined times as succession or measurement of moments or length of time. Time here is the length of time to finish the process. This is the completion of time or a season designated by God for the return of Jesus to catch away his bride when restoration of all things has completed its course.

Praise the Lord! We will be out of here.

The sad thing about this is only those who loves, repents and converts, and have their sins under the blood of Jesus are going with Jesus. This is why we need to understand the spiritual seasons of God. We cannot just casually go through life from spiritual seasons doing as we please totally ignoring the spiritual seasons of spiritual development.

CHAPTER 5

CYCLES OF SEASONS

Cycle # 1. The Law of Seasons

The first cycle we must know is that each season of God is under His law. Each season was set in order by the Omnipotent, Sovereign rule of God at creation. God is the author, designer, and judge of seasons. He watches over His word to perform it (Jeremiah 1:12). Therefore, can we be ignorant, complacent, or disobedient to achieve all the potential blessings contained in new seasons. NO! God's law of sowing and reaping is always in effect. If we do not fulfill a new season, we will not reap the blessings, victories, maturing, and peace and joy provided by God in each new spiritual season.

Psalms 37:23
The steps of a good man are ordered by the Lord, and He delights in his way.

Hebrew definition of ordered is fixed, established, made ready. The main idea is to bring something into incontrovertible existence (nothing or anyone can change). Our journey through life is already set in order to travel through spiritual seasons. If we get out of step or time with God's plans for our life, we are breaking His law and we will suffer for our disobedience.

Ecclesiastes 8:2-6

I say, "Keep the king's commandment for the sake of your oath to God. Do not be hasty to go from his presence. Do not take your stand for an evil thing, for he does whatever pleases Him."

Where the word of a king is, there is power, and who may say to him, "What are you doing?" He who keeps his command will experience nothing harmful, and a wise man's heart discerns both time and judgment because for every matter there is a time and judgment though the misery of man increases greatly.

Judgment is defined as a verdict or a sentence that is favorable or unfavorable.

God has already judged and pronounced a verdict on each new season. When we fail to obey, the verdict is already given and we leave God's blessings and fall under His cursing. This is automatic. He has already spoken. This verdict has a two fold sentence:

1. To miss out on all that God has planned for our benefit and pleasure in each new season.
2. The demise of one will affect the rest of the body we are connected to. Each person in the body is intricately a part of God's Kingdom and to a local body.

At each new season, we are required by God and held accountable for performing the part we are created to do. Our failure will affect others and also affect our own life.

Esther 4:14

For if you remain completely silent at this time (the right time, a short-lived season, the proper time) relief and deliverance will arise from the Jews from another place, but you and your father's house will perish. Yet who knows whether you have come to the Kingdom for such a time (same Hebrew word) as this.

Esther and her father's house would have perished under God's judgment.

The word time is the same Hebrew word used in Ecclesiastes 3:1, that is defined as a set time or season. We are required by God to function in our purpose for each new season or we will suffer God's judgment.

Don't you think you should spend more time pleasing God and less time pleasing self? God said it. It is law. We must agree with Him.

Cycle #2. The Cycle of Spiritual Growth

Each season contains the seeds of potential for spiritual growth.

Acts 17:28
In Him we live and move and have our being;

In Him is when we enter the life of the new seed. Move is when we are traveling through life walking in His steps that are already prepared for us. Have our being is maturing and becoming like Christ.

One cannot enter the life of a new seed and not change.

Change is imminent. God has planned each season with His wisdom and power to enable us to have spiritual maturity and development. When we accept Christ as our personal Savior, we enter into His Kingdom as a baby. However, as His comparison to the natural realm of maturing from a baby to an adult is the example to also grow as a spiritual baby to a full son of God. If we do not recognize the spiritual transformation of our spirits in each season of God, we will never achieve the fullness of God nor become the mature sons of God. We will remain as spiritual babies.

Galatians 4:1
Now I say that the heir, as long as he is a child will remain in bondage to the system of the world because the child doesn't possess the ability or knowledge to take authority and break free.

I Corinthians 3:1
As for me, brothers, I couldn't talk to you as spiritual people but as worldly people, as babies, so far as experience with Jesus is concerned. I gave you milk, not solid food, because you were not ready for it.

Again, here is another analogy of the natural body and the spiritual body. A baby can't eat solid food and a spiritual baby cannot eat the strong meat of the word or do spiritual warfare or take it's rightful place in the body of Christ or society.

I Peter 2:2
Be like newborn babies, thirsty for pure milk of the word so that by it, you may grow up into deliverance.

Thirsty or desire is written in the imperative mood which is a command. God is commanding us to be thirsty or to desire the word so that we can grow into maturity and be like Him.

II Corinthians 3:17-18
Now the Lord is the spirit; and where the Spirit of the Lord is, there is liberty. But we all, with unveiled face, beholding as in a mirror, the glory of the Lord are being transformed into the same image from glory to glory, just as by the spirit of the Lord.

Transformation is written in the contemporaneous action which is defined as an action happening in the same period of time of the encounter.

Changes of maturity will only come when we are face to face with what God wants to accomplish in each season.

God has planned for our spiritual growth in each spiritual season, as long as we remain a spiritual baby, we cannot be the salt and light to the world, ambassadors of God, disciples, ministers, leaders, intercessors, prayer warriors, a threat to the enemy or witnesses to the world. How disappointing to God this must be. Even though we love babies in the natural realm, we still want them to grow up and become more like us.

Dr. Caroline Leaf said, "Every moment of every day you are changing your brain with your thoughts in a positive or negative direction. Every time you think or make a choice, you cause structural change in your brain. By controlling the direction of your mind, you control the direction of your life."

This is great. Shouldn't we be thinking more about the spiritual realm? Would this keep our brain more healthy? I believe so. Could this keep us from the diseases of the brain? I believe so.

Cycle #3. Initiate Change

New seasons create an atmosphere conducive to change. It creates a pattern or expected change. Seasons present change as normal activity and sets a premises of a continued process.

Change is imminent. The definition and nature of seasons demands change. Each natural season demands a change in climate, weather, activities, clothing, education, travel, and food. Spiritual seasons also have patterns that demand change in our thinking, mindsets, actions, talking, living, spiritual maturity, prayer life, and more. Just as we expect and welcome new seasons in the natural, we should do the same in the spiritual. However, some Christians never want to change. They are concrete Christians, set in their ways and resist change in themselves and for others.

II Peter 3:18
Grow in grace and knowledge of our Lord and Savior Jesus Christ.

Grow is defined as increase. One cannot increase without change. *One cannot enter the life of a new season and not change. A new season is a seed from God.*

The fruition of a seed demands change. Changes also create an excitement for a closure of one season and an entrance into the next season. This excitement of change keeps us on a continued journey through life from season to season.

It creates a motivation in us to not set on the sidelines of life watching the world go by, but encourages us to be a participant in the process.

I had a dream that I was leading a group of people on a journey to reach the top of a mountain. The top of the mountain was our final destination, because it had a great blessing waiting on us. As we journeyed toward the mountain, we came up on an older man sitting on a bench with his back toward the mountain. I looked at his face and it looked so long, unhappy, and sad. He had lost hope and turned his back to the mountain and set down on his dreams of reaching his destiny. I encouraged the people and we continued on our journey toward the mountain. Change is eminent or mandatory to reach our destiny of the eternal realm of God.

Matthew 10:22
And you will be hated by all on account of my name. But it is the one who endures to the end who will be saved.

Cycle #4. Set time

God, and His eternal realm, is outside of time and is not limited to time, but He has set seasons of time for His specific purposes and watches over them with His watchful eyes. His throne sets over the world in His eternal spiritual realm outside of time, therefore, He sees the beginning and the end of the same time period. The higher you go, the more of the lower level you will be able to see.

God in His infinite wisdom has set seasons, with a set time frame, from the beginning of time to the end of time for the benefit and pleasure for man. Only God knows the duration of a spiritual season. A season can be a moment, minute, hour, day, week, month, or years.

Principles of Set Times.

Principle #1. Set times have past, present, future.

Set times have a beginning and an ending. One needs to know the voice of the Holy Spirit to tell them the beginning or have spiritual discernment to discern the beginning of seasons.

The wise old saying in discerning the beginning or ending of natural seasons is, "you can feel it in the air." Well, if you are sensitive to the Holy Spirit you can feel the beginning of the spiritual seasons in the air. Also, the prophets start prophesying about the new seasons, and the apostle establishes the new season in the earth.

Amos 3:7
Surely the Lord God does nothing, unless He reveals His secret to the servants the prophets.

Ephesians 2:20
Having been built on the foundation of the apostles and prophets, Jesus Christ Himself being the chief cornerstone.

It is very important to enter the new season at its beginning so you are not behind trying to catch up. Also, you need the foundation of the beginning to add the new dimension to your spiritual house.

Staying current with what God is presently doing keeps you on the cutting edge or front line of His will. By being in the present, you are not only enjoying His presence, but you are preparing for your future.

You are eating fresh bread from Heaven instead of eating stale bread of the past. You are beholding His face and going forward instead of looking at His back where He has already been. You are walking in His presence and becoming one with Him in voice and walk.

Principle #2. Your Future

If you have successfully completed the beginning and the present of a season, you are ready to walk in the maturity of the change. I believe God and His perfect plan gives us a time to put into practice and become doers of the word of the new season before He launches us into a new season. This is a special time to enjoy the fruit of your labor.

I remember when I finished my Bible College ahead of schedule and how happy I was. I wasn't happy because I was out of school, but because of all that I had learned and accomplished.

The satisfaction and joy of achieving your goal of finishing a season is beyond expression. The thrill of victory of overcoming every obstacle and temptation to quit, given by the Devil. You won the battle. Praise the Lord! Enjoy walking in the new level with God.

Principle #3 – Affects your Destiny

Each new season is a part of your destiny and is a determining factor in how you will arrive at it. In what stage of maturity will you be when you arrive at your destiny? What kind of treasure are you laying up in Heaven? Which time frame are you living in? Where do you fit in the new season? Where do you fit in the body of Christ? The Holy Spirit asked me these questions, so, I am asking you, by the Holy Spirit, the same questions. Everyone needs to ask themselves these questions. II Corinthians 13:5 commands us to examine and test ourselves.

Psalm 119:59-60
I thought about my ways and I turned my feet toward Your instructions. I hurry, I don't delay, to keep your commandments.

We need to think about our way, what we are saying and doing, to see if we are pleasing God. *Your destiny depends on how you manage the time and season.*

If a season has finished its course and we still remain in it, we will suffer from being out of God's presence and His will. We will remain a relic of the past. If we jump ahead of God into our future before the present season has ended, we will either fall flat in our efforts or create an Ishmael. Either one is outside of God's will and is dead works without any reward. After you have successfully completed a season, you are eligible for a promotion in the body of Christ and in the spiritual realm.

You may not be promoted to a new position, however, you will be recognized and respected in the body as being more like Christ. Also, you will be respected in the spiritual realm of Satan as having more authority.

Acts 19:13-14
Seven sons of Sceva tried to cast out evil spirits from some people and the spirit spoke to the sons and said, "Jesus I know, and Paul I know, but who are you?"

The sons were not recognized in the evil kingdom of darkness as having the power and authority to tell the evil spirits what to do. The Devil knows who we are, what we have done, and what we are qualified to do in the spiritual realm.

Principle #4 – Being at the Right Place at the Right Time.

This is Satan's most productive plan against humanity. If we are off the right step or on the right step but out of time being there, we miss out on what God has planned for us in this season. The bottom line of being in the right place at the right time is to buy, possess, and take ownership of time.

Ephesians 5:15-16
See then that you will walk circumspectly, not as fools, but as wise, redeeming the time, because the days are evil.

Redeeming is defined as to buy up and not to allow the suitable moment to pass by unheeded, but make it one's own. In order to do this, these principles of success must be followed.

- *Place a value on time.*

How much do we value time? What is it worth to you? What are you willing to sacrifice for it?

The less value you place on something the less you are willing to sacrifice for it. Is time nothing to you and eternity everything or is time everything and eternity nothing?

How much do we want to please God? If eternity is everything, we must move to qualify ourselves to go there. How much passion for God do we have? Everyone has the same time limit of twenty-four hours a day and seven days a week. Do not steal time from someone else by being late for any appointment or schedule.

If you cause someone to wait for you by being late, you have stolen their time and are classified as a thief. You will reap what you sow. Have respect for others and their time.

Time should be elevated to the highest priced commodity we value.

- ***Purchase time.***

Make the decision and take the first step and die to self and totally sell out to God. Each person must make a declaration or confession to take possession of time. What you do not own, you will not take total care for it. Then, each person must make a declaration or confession of placing the Holy Spirit in charge of your life to direct your steps as you walk.

Acts 1:7-8
It is not for you to know the times and the season which the Father set by His own authority. But you shall receive power when the Holy Spirit has come up on you, and you shall be witnesses to the me in Jerusalem, and in all Judea and Samaria, and to the end of the earth.

We do not know our next step to take, but the Holy Spirit does and He will lead us to walk in them. This is the only way we can be at the right place at the right time. God in His perfect plan for man has already prepared your steps to walk through your whole life from the beginning to the end.

Ephesians 2:10
For we are His workmanship, created in Christ Jesus for good works, which God prepared beforehand that we shall walk in them.

The disciples asked Jesus about a time and Jesus answered, "It is not for you to know times and seasons." Only God knows because they are under His authority. Usually, we stop after this verse and preach, we are not supposed to know the times of God.

However, Jesus continues with the next verse that we preach about going to all of the world and totally separate these two verses to have different meanings. Yet, Jesus is continuing His instructions to answer the disciple's question. Jesus is saying we cannot know in our natural infinite minds, but the Holy Spirit has the power, authority, and leadership you need to travel through life locally and to the whole world, then you will be at the right place at the right time to do the right purpose. You can't serve two masters at the same time.

The law of physics says that two objects cannot occupy the same space at the same time.

When we are obeying God we cannot obey the Devil and when we are obeying the Devil we cannot obey God. We cannot walk the steps prepared by God and walk with the Devil in his steps at the same time. Neither can we be where God created us to be and be at the place the Devil has lured us to be, at the same time. Therefore, we must be led by the Holy Spirit to know when we are supposed to be in Jerusalem (your local residence), Judah (your surrounding area and to the rest of the world)

- *Prioritize your time.*

You cannot own time unless you prioritize it. If you do not prioritize, time will own you. You will fall as a victim and be out of place at the wrong time. God is in the eternal realm, but He placed man in the time realm and gave him dominion to rule over it. Satan is a thief and he wants to steal time from you so that you will be out of place at God's appointed time for your life. *Prioritizing time is allowing the Holy Spirit to direct you in making your schedule.*

Psalms 31:15
My times are in your hand. Deliver me from the hand of my enemies.

II Timothy 4:2
Preach the word. Be ready in season and out of season. Convince, rebuke, encourage with great patience and every kind of instruction.

Be ready is written in the imperative mood which is a command from God. The definition is to stand by, be present, be at hand which implies being at the right place at the right time.

Acts 8:26-40
This is a great lesson about Philip and the Eunuch.

They both had a purpose for meeting each other at the right place at the right time. The Eunuch needed an answer and Phillip had the answer. Phillip led him to Jesus and baptized him and the Holy Spirit transported Phillip in the spirit. They both had a great experience and a blessing by being at the right place at the right time. John Chapter 11 is a great teaching from God. Jesus receives the news about His special friend, Lazarus, being sick. Jesus told the disciples He needed to go to Judah to see His friend. Listen to the disciples respond. "We are afraid to go."

Jesus answered, "If anyone walks in the day, he will not stumble, because he sees the light of this world, but if one walks in the night, he stumbles, because the light is not in him,"

WHAT is Jesus saying? What if Jesus said that to you? Walking in the light represents walking in the revealed steps of God and walking in the dark represents walking out of the revealed steps of God.

Walking in the light represents walking in your future which is already planned by God. Walking in the dark represents walking out of His steps of your future and ending up in failure. *Walking in darkness is walking blindly in your future.* We end up out of place and out of time in God's seasons. Jesus knew what He was supposed to do, but the disciples did not know because they were not led by the Holy Spirit. They tried to persuade Jesus from being at the right place at the right time.

Security men and women who are hired to protect the malls and business are required to walk in prepared steps, and they are to punch a clock at each station to prove they were at the right place at the right time or they will be fired. If we do not walk at the right place at the right time, we are not walking one with God. Therefore, we will not fully receive His blessings.

We must own time or time will own you. To own time is to achieve the full potential in each moment.

Time will slip away so quickly and is gone never to be rebought or relived. Whatever you missed you cannot recall, because whatever was due to happen in God's plan for you cannot be relived.

I was invited to minister at this place and the Holy Spirit told me to go. The Holy Spirit spoke to me to tell the story of a woman asking me to pray for her sister that had cancer and she was healed. After this service, another lady came up to Phyllis and me to ask us to pray for her daughter-in-law.

She told us it was God talking to her when she heard me tell the story. Her daughter-in-law was diagnosed with a condition that would led to death. She was crying while she was telling us. We prayed and believed for her miracle.

A few weeks later, I was at another place and this lady walked up to me and said, "Do you remember me?" I responded with a yes, but I do not recall your name. She told me her daughter-in-law called and said she was confused and did not know what to do. She said I went to the doctor for treatment and he told me he couldn't find anything wrong with me. The lady started crying and praising the Lord while telling me the story. She said her daughter-in-law did not believe in healing and she did not tell her we had prayed for her healing. Now, she could explain healing to her.

All this happened because we were at the right place at the right time. The Holy Spirit instructed me to go minister, the lady obeyed God and went to the meeting, the Holy Spirit told me to tell the story of a lady being healed, this lady was bold enough to ask us to pray for her daughter-in-law and she was miraculously healed because the leading of the Holy Spirit. What would have happened if either one of us failed to be at the right place at the right time?

Each moment of time carries a new purpose. So, how much value do you put on each new moment? Everyone has twenty-four hours a day and seven days a week to manage your time. How much time do you give to please God and how much time do you give to please yourself? If time is nothing and eternity everything? Do you believe the eternal realm of God is more important than pleasing self? What are you going to do about it?

Your future is now and what you do today is preparing your future.

So, shouldn't we take more time to please God today than to please ourselves with pleasures of life to prepare our eternal life with Him? Time is short and eternity is never ending! We should be preparing to go there and less time staying here.

The eternal realm consists of two places, Heaven or Hell and we are going to be in one or the other depending on what we are doing in time. We should be preparing for the eternal realm of Heaven with God.

This example summarizes being at the right place at the right time, placing a value on time, purchasing time, and prioritizing time. While in my prayer time, the Holy Spirit spoke to me to go on a cruise. Boy! Was I excited! Finally a mission trip my wife and I could enjoy as a vacation without doing a lot of warfare and battling the enemy. The first full day, after filling our plates at the breakfast buffet, we were looking for a table to sit and eat. There were no empty tables so I asked this couple to sit with them. They were Christians, very nice, and a pleasure to talk to.

The next day, the same thing happened with the same couple. The Holy Spirit spoke to Phyllis and she asked them if we could meet them later to pray and minister to them. They agreed. They showed us a graduation picture of their son and he was a very nice looking young man. She showed us another picture of him without a shirt and he didn't look like the same person.

He was skin and bones with tattoos and piercings all over his body. His mother was crying and asked us to pray for him because he was addicted to drugs. We prayed and did warfare over him and Phyllis gave her a prophecy that he was coming home and surrendering his life back to God. I gave her a word to start a home fellowship. She cried and said this was what she felt to do but she was afraid she couldn't do it.

Two weeks after we returned home, she called crying and praising the Lord and said her son came home and gave his heart back to God and they were going to start a home fellowship.

This has been over four years ago and they are doing great. We had to be on the right ship at the right time and be willing to spend $3,000.00 for one soul and start a new work for God.

If we want to please God, be His ambassador, and represent Him, and be in the right season. We must be totally surrendered to His will to sacrifice at all costs.

Cycle# 5. God's purpose for the Season.

God's purpose for the season is the most important reason for the season. What is God saying? What does God want to do? What does God want to accomplish in us? Nothing exists without purpose. Without a purpose, there would be no season. *All the cycles hang on the purpose.*

Purpose becomes the head, the control center, and with everything else hanging onto it. When purpose of God's will comes first, everything else falls into place. Man was created by God for His fellowship and everything else was created for man.

Matthew 25:14-30, God gives everyone a gift, talent or call which represents purpose, and He holds us accountable for it and stewards over it.

I Peter 4:10.
As each one has received a gift, minister it to one another, as good stewards of the manifold grace of God.

Different seasons are developing tools used by God to develop and qualify us for the eternal realm with Him. However, if we bury our purpose in the ground, we disqualify ourselves.

Burying our purpose in the ground is burying it in our own self will or the part of us God created from the dust of earth.

Skipping seasons by ignorance or rebellion is like skipping grades in school. The one skipping is the one who suffers loss. Timing is so important to our purpose. Are we ready when God says its time or have we missed the timing of God and disqualified our self because of selfish motives? Did we move when God said move or were there things we wanted to accomplish for ourselves first? Our motives have to be right when we change seasons.

When God gives us instructions for His plan, do we accept it as a servant, eager to do God's will, or do we look at it as an opportunity to promote self. God speaks and we need to listen when He speaks and not procrastinate and wait until we think we are ready.

When God calls you, He will qualify you if you will make the first step as He guides and instructs you.

Cycle #6. Instant in Season and out of Season

II Timothy 4:2.
Preach the word. Be ready in season and out of season. Convince, rebuke, exhort, with all patience and instruction.

At first glance at this scripture, it seems to be an oxymoron. If you are in a season, then how can you be out of a season?

Let's break down this scripture's meaning. First, the words proclaim, instant, correct, and exhort are all written in the imperative mood which means a command. God is speaking through Apostle Paul to young Timothy and commanding him to do these things. He is not giving him an option. We are all commanded to share the Truth.

The definition of instant is to stand by, be present, be at hand. It has an application of being ready or prepared at any moment to represent Him.

We went to Washington D.C. to do a prayer walk. It was cold and I was all bundled up to stay warm. We stayed on the outskirts of D.C. and was riding the Metro to the Capitol Building. It was Saturday and the metro wasn't busy so I asked the attendant for the best schedule. She was African American and I am Caucasian. She helped me and she said, "you are a pastor." This took me by surprise because I didn't have anything on that would identify me as a pastor. She asked me to pray for her sister who had cancer and I did. I took her hand, while standing in the middle of the Metro station, and prayed. I prayed the prayer from my spirit and she felt it. She said she believed her sister was healed.

I am ready to pray whenever asked. I asked the question about being in season and out of season as an oxymoron. The definition of the first season is an appropriate time or well-timed. The definition of the second season is an inappropriate time. When you leave a season of God and enter into the next season of God, this is a progressive process.

However, even though you are in a new season and the old season has been completed, you can still proclaim the truth of the old season that you have learned. You may encounter someone unexpectedly or unplanned that is still in the old season that needs the truth expounded and you can be ready to help them because you have already learned and experienced the past seasons of God.

I Peter 3:15
But sanctify the Lord God in your hearts, and always be ready to give an answer to everyone who asks you a reason for the hope that is in you, with meekness and fear.

Everyone needs to be ready to be bold as a lion to give an answer to everyone who asks.

This is the season to allow the roar of the lion of the tribe of Judah (Jesus) to roar through us louder than the roar of the devil against you.

Always be ready to help or give encouragement to others.

Cycle #7. Evict the devil from the New Season.

There are many different teachings, theories, and doctrines about Satan and his kingdom of darkness. Only a few are correct and truthful. The rest are a lie and untruthful. Only the truth will set you free but all untruth will bring you into bondage and darkness. So, do you want the truth? Let's start from the beginning of time and take a journey through history. God created Adam and Eve and placed them in the Garden of Eden to rule the world but they listened to Satan and obeyed him instead of obeying God. They did not evict Satan from the Garden as they should have since those were the rules. Therefore, God evicted them. By obeying Satan, they gave him the victory and the title of God of this world and became servants of him.

God started the Redemption process of restoring the fallen man, therefore patterns developed. God gave land back to them called The Promised Land or The Land of Israel. He gave the pattern of taking control of the land by driving out the enemy from the land little by little. They drove out the enemy only as they advanced and moved forward. God gave them the ability, power, and the authority to defeat the enemy but they had to physically take action and battle the enemy and drive them from the land. This was the natural realm.

Today, we deal with evil spirits in the spiritual realm. When Jesus defeated the devil at the cross, he didn't evict him from the earth or bind him, but He left him on earth to devour anyone who will allow him to do it.(1 Peter 5:8) We must clear the devil from each new level of spiritual advancement we make and take the territory God is giving us.

We must follow the pattern of the second Adam(Jesus). Jesus, the Son of God, came to earth to die on the cross to redeem man back to God. Jesus was a man just like us and He set the pattern to defeat Satan and take back the crown of ruler of the earth.

Let's look at the pattern Jesus used to enter His New Season of Ministry:

Pattern #1. Jesus left the Past Season.
He went to the River of Jordan to be baptized. Why? *Jesus set the pattern to enter new seasons.* Even though He had not sinned, He still wanted to be free of the past. Baptism provides the removal of the past and a new beginning of life. At the beginning of the new season, we are to ask Jesus to forgive and cleanse us from all unrighteousness, of all the things we have done, said, thought, or failed to do. We cannot carry all of our failures, allegiances, shortcomings into the new season. The pull of the past will be too hard to push forward in the new season.

Pattern #2. Jesus was led by the Holy Spirit.
Jesus was our example. Remember, Jesus said He only did what He saw His Father do, and He only said what He heard His Father say. So, Jesus did not know all the future. He had to be led by the Holy Spirit. We do not see the steps of our future that God has already made for us unless the Holy Spirit reveals them to us.

John 16:13
But when He, the spirit of truth, comes He will guide you into all truth for He will not speak of His own authority, but whatever He hears He will speak and tell you things to come.

The Holy Spirit lead Jesus into the wilderness to be tempted by the Devil. Matthew 4:1. If we are too become mature, take possession of our life and become like Jesus, we must conquer and evict the enemy of our soul, and only the Holy Spirit knows the time and place for the battle.

Pattern #3. Jesus defeated Satan's Temptations.
Remember, at this time, Jesus had not defeated Satan at the cross. He was a man just like you and me. Jesus was led by the Holy Spirit into the dry, hot desert land that had no water or vegetation. After he had fasted forty days, the devil came to him and said, "If you are the Son of God, command that the stones become bread." The Devil was trying to steal the word from Jesus. Jesus heard God shout from Heaven at His baptism that He was God's beloved son. When the Holy Spirit speaks to us, Satan tries to steal the written word or the prophetic word from us.

A. Temptation #1

<u>**The Devil attacked Jesus' Body.**</u>

The body has five senses and each one provides a pleasure that is either good or bad. We can see all the pleasures of the world, feel all the pleasures of the world, taste all the pleasures of the world, hear all of the pleasures of the world, and smell all the pleasures of the world. All the bad, negative things: porno, sex, drugs, alcohol, dirty talk, dirty worldly music, smell of evil things, lie, cheat, steal, murder, and all of the works of the flesh. The Devil tempted Jesus with food because he hadn't eat in forty days. Jesus makes a powerful statement.

Matthew 4:4
"Man shall not live by bread alone, but by every word that proceed out of the mouth of God."

John 6:35
Jesus is the bread of life.

He was and is the Word and He elevated the Word (truth) above the desires of His body. Jesus did not let His body control Him and neither can we. Our body has to be under the control of our spirit to be like Jesus.

B. Temptation #2

The Devil attacking Jesus' Soul

The Devil takes Jesus to the top of a high mountain overlooking Jericho. He showed Jesus all of the kingdoms of the world and their glory. Jericho was a beautiful and important city offering the pleasures of life. Some people say the Devil did not have the world to offer but he did. Adam gave it to him when he obeyed him instead of God. All Jesus had to do was worship the Devil. The soul contains all of the emotions that releases all of the pleasures of the world and all the vain glory of exalted self. Jesus said, "Get the behind me Satan for it is written you shall worship the Lord your God, in Him alone you shall serve." Never take the easy road out, but always put God first. Adam obeyed the Devil and exalted himself and lost everything.

C. Temptation #3

The Devil attacking Jesus' Spirit.

The Devil took Jesus to the holy city of Jerusalem and set Him on the pinnacle and said, "if you are the son of God, throw yourself down. For it is written: He shall give His angels charge over you. In their hands, they shall bear you up, lest you dash your foot against a stone." In the heart of Israel at the religious center of the world, the Devil targets Jesus. The Devil was trying to get Jesus to do a religious act on His own and not by the Spirit. Then, Jesus could not have said, I only obey God.

We create acts of the flesh by doing things for God we have not been instructed to do.

The deceiving Devil is tempting Jesus to obey him instead of God thus nullifying the sinless second Adam. Jesus would have disqualified himself as Messiah, the savior of the world and redeemer of man, if He had acted in his soul(self) instead of His spirit. Jesus defeated the devil in all the areas of man: spirit, soul, and body. Jesus defeated the full temptation of Satan while operating as a human being.

Now, after Jesus defeated Satan at the cross, stripped him of the crown of God of this world, gave us His name, and gave us the Holy Spirit. We should be able to easily defeat Satan ourselves. We have to evict the devil from each new season because each new season takes us into a higher realm of God. Satan has entered the first and second Heaven and his ranking spirits are in control. So, with each new realm we reach, we have to drive out the spirit of Satan. Why is there so much confusion about the devil? He is a liar and exploits this character trait to his advantage. As long as people believe the lies about him, it produces a camouflage screen around him and protects him while he mocks us.

There are many false teachings about Satan and we cannot believe them. The Bible says, believe a lie and be damned. The definition of damned is to separate, to condemn, to judge. When you are damned, you are separated from the truth and you are judged to bondage and captivity. Jesus defeated the devil at the cross and stripped him of his title of god of this world. If Jesus had obeyed Satan, He would have received a self-righteous spirit from the devil and He could not have gone to the cross. The definition of self-righteous is a strong belief that your own actions, opinions, righteousness are right and others are wrong. Jesus would have operated out of His soul instead of His spirit. This action by-passes God and exalts self, and the devil would have defeated Him. Yet, God did not lock Satan up, bind him, or send him somewhere away from man. God allowed him to stay and roam around earth seeking whom he may devour?

I Peter 5:8
Yet, at the end time, God will send an angel and chain and lock up Satan for 1,000 years.

Until then, according to I John 5:19, the whole world lies under the power of the evil one.

Cycle #8. Process of Assimilation.

Definition – To take in and incorporate as one's own, to become like others. The process of taking in and absorbing into the mind and fully understanding information, ideas, and expressions. Likeness or similarity, to become like others. Second meaning is assimilation of food into the body.

Our Responsibility of Assimilation

- *Observing and Learning*

As a trained leader in both secular and Christian institutions, I am very observant of everything happening around me in the natural realm and the Spiritual realm. I try to look through the eyes of the Holy Spirit to observe the location I am in, building, atmosphere, workers, organization, attitudes, friendliness, welcome, speakers, worship, music, spiritual activity, maturity level, servant hearts, and what is being said to glean whatever He wants me to receive. We cannot bury our heads in the sand, walk blindly through this life or have a deaf ear to what the world is saying if we want to be a quality representative of God.

Recently, after attending two great meetings, I asked the Holy Spirit what I was to take back home with me to implement in my life and my church because I always look to become more like Christ in everything I do. It is the wrong Biblical pattern to think we cannot receive from someone else or think we are better or more qualified than others. No one is the full stature and image of Jesus Christ so we all need to continue to change. Yet, at the same time, we cannot be gullible and believe everything we hear and see without prayer and meditation. While lying in bed in a hotel room after the great meetings, I had a special meeting with the Holy Spirit. He spoke to me the word, assimilation, and dropped into me a special word about assimilation that the body of Christ is missing.

Our duty and responsibility of assimilation is taking the truth which we hear or read and turning it into the life of Jesus in ourselves. As we become more like Him, we will become the full image and stature of Jesus.

Ephesians 4:12-13
For the perfecting of the saints, for the work of the ministry, for the edifying of the body of Christ:

Til we all come in the unity of the faith, and of the knowledge of the son of God and to the perfect man, and to the measure of the stature of the fullness of Christ.

This should be our daily work.

- *Pattern of Assimilation.*

Assimilation in the natural realm is the body, and assimilation in the spiritual realm, is the spirit.

I Corinthians 15:45-49
And so it is written, the first man Adam was made a living soul; the last Adam was made a quickening spirit.

Howbeit that was not first which is spiritual, but that which is natural; and afterward that which is spiritual.

The first man is of the earth, earthy: the second man is the Lord from Heaven.

And is this earthy, such are they also that are earthy; and as is the heavenly, such are they also that are heavenly.

And as we have borne the image of the earthy, we shall also bear the image of the heavenly.

People do not understand how the spiritual realm works so God illustrates the natural realm first to give us a clear picture of how the spiritual realm works. We understand the natural realm of eating food to nourish our bodies through assimilation and the spiritual realm works the same way. Assimilation is applied in both the natural man or the body and the spiritual man or the spirit. Both were created by God. The natural man has a body made from dust and the spiritual man has a body created from the breath of God.

The spiritual body is inside the natural body. The spiritual body looks just like the natural body and has some functions like the natural body.

The spiritual body has a mind, ears, speaks, tastes, and has the appearance of the natural body. After Jesus raised from the dead, He appeared in His spiritual body and He was recognized as Jesus. He walked through walls, would appear and disappear. The stomach of the natural man is the processor of assimilation of natural food. The Holy Spirit is the processor of assimilation of spiritual food.

I Peter 2:2
John 6:32-35
Romans 12:1-2

The Bible is clear that the word of God is food for the spirit. Just as natural food is essential for the natural body to grow and live so is the spiritual body dependent on spiritual food to sustain growth and live. Comparing assimilation in the natural realm one cannot eat everything you see or is available because some food is not good for you and will bring harm to you. Neither can we listen to anyone who is teaching fake doctrines. False doctrines is a lie and a lie brings judgment, dominion, and captivity to you.

I Corinthians 2:9-12

But as it is written, eye have not seen nor ear heard, neither have entered into the heart of man the things of which God hath prepared for them that love him.

But God hath revealed them unto us by His spirit; for the Spirit searches all things; yea, the deep things of God.

For what man knows the things of a man, except the spirit of man which is in him? Even so no one knows the things of God except the Spirit of God.

Now we have received, not the spirit of the world, but the Spirit who is from God, that we might know the things that are freely given to us by God.

The definition of revealed is to make known. The scripture text states, has revealed indicating the information was made known in the past. However, the word revealed is written in the aorist tense which has no past, present, or future tense.

So, when did the Holy Spirit reveal or make known the text? I believe that God, before creation, and before time revealed to the Holy Spirit all things in the eternal realm to make known to man in the times and seasons of God. This is why God tells us to own time. To own the fullness of time requires an intimate relationship with the Holy Spirit because only He can reveal God's plan for each moment. The Bible says that the Holy Spirit will guide us John 16:13. Not only is the Holy Spirit the voice of God to reveal His will but also is the one who assimilates of the truth to fill the spiritual body to cause spiritual growth.

Holy Spirit assimilates the truth of God and turns it into the life of Jesus so we can become more like Him.

God wants us to develop His character, integrity, power, authority, humility, fruit of the spirit, and His likeness, so we can become a true ambassador, salt, and light to the world.

- *Opening Four Gates*

In order to assimilate the truth, we must have input of truth through the gates of the nature body.

Gate #1. Ear, Eye, and Touch Gates.

The word enters the eye and ear gates and is received by the brain. In order to turn the word into bread, the word must reach the spirit. If the brain does not retain what you hear or read, then you must write it down or play it again or type it so you will not lose it.

Gate #2. Process of Meditation.

You then meditate on the word you have received and revelation and understanding

Proverbs 23:7
For as he *thinks* in his heart, so is he.

Definition of *thinks* is to open, to act as a gatekeeper, to think.

The city gate was where the people congregated for business and social reasons. The administration of justice was often administered at the gate. It was the place of controlled access to a walled city. What is God saying? What you open to your heart, you become. Meditation is opening the gate of your heart so the revelation can come into your walled mindset. Meditation is the gatekeeper of information coming into your spirit.

You become what you mediate on.

Gate #3. The next step is confession

You are instructed to confess or declare the word with your mouth. Confessing the word brings the seed from the brain and the mind and plants a seed into your spirit.
The Holy Spirit assimilates the seed into the life of Christ in your spirit and likeness of God is produced.
As your spirit is fed, it will grow into the likeness of God. Your spirit will grow from a baby, who cannot rule, into the fall stature and image of God. You will be able to rule as a king in God's Kingdom. Your spirit will rule you, your soul, and body, and you will walk victoriously as you journey through life. The roar of the lion of the tribe of Judah from your spirit will be louder and more powerful than the roar of the devil against you.
A mature spirit will produce the roar of a lion but a starved, weak spirit will only produce a meow from a kitty cat.
When the process takes place, you will be able to rule your domain and sphere of influence with your purpose in life.

Gate #4. Desire Activities the Seed of Life.

Proverbs 13:12
But when desire comes, it is a tree of life.

Definition of desire is a craving, longing, that compels to the attainment or possession of something, either good, delightful or bad. This word can be used in a negative or positive way. Desire gives birth to the seed of good or evil.

Desire filtered through the emotions of the soul produces a tree or knowledge of good and evil. Desire filtered through the spirit produces a tree of life and fruit of the spirit.

Desire starts out as a craving for something then proceeds into a tree that produces fruit, either the works of the devil or the works of God. *Everything starts with a desire then you have a choice to act upon that desire.*

An action or an expression of words plants a seed and if the process is not stopped, it will produce a full grown manifestation of the life of the seed. You now will eat the fruit of your lips and reap what you sowed. When your spirit is in control of your life, your love for Jesus will cause you to burn for His truth like His disciples on the road to Emmaus. The words of Jesus burned in their hearts.

Luke 24:13-25 – this desire will keep the desire of the soul from influencing you to create an act of the flesh and become bound to sin. Since desire contains both the negative and positive potential, discernment is required to determine the origin of desire as to whether it is coming from the body (lust of flesh), soul (exalting self) or from the spirit (representing God).

<u>Cycle #9: Leaving and Entering.</u>

Leaving and Entering is one of the most important patterns in the Bible. It all started when Adam and Eve had to leave the Garden of Eden when they disobeyed God because disobedience is sin. Before man could enter restoration from the sin,

Jesus(the second Adam) had to take Adam's sin to the cross and remove the sin, by shedding His blood, then man could enter the new season of being restored to God. A cycle or a pattern was initiated by God and we must follow this cycle. Before we enter a new season, we must ask for forgiveness of any failure, disobedience, sin, mindsets, thoughts, non-destiny activities, or sins of omission. These things cannot enter the new season or the pull of the past will act like a giant rubber band to stop our forward progress; then it will pull us back into the same old habits, limitations, patterns, and struggles of life. Each new season is a process from God to change and mature us into the full image of Christ so we can qualify ourselves as sons of God.

As we mature and cut off all the old Adam, we enter into the inner circle with God and back to the Garden of His blessings and happiness.

I have written a book titled, "Leaving and Entering" that explains all about this process. You can purchase the book from me or Amazon.

CHAPTER 6

LAST SEASON

Part One: Visions and Dreams God Showed Me

Only God knows the time He has set to end the world. However, He has given us signs in the Bible to allow us to see the closeness of His plans for the end, just like we have road signs in the natural to reveal the distances to our destinations. I believe we have entered the last major season of time and we are nearing our destination.

A little over three years ago, the Lord gave me a vision and several dreams that He wanted me to fulfill. I saw myself pushing a baby carriage with nothing in it and I was headed to a high mountain that was on the horizon, a long distance away. Several years ago, the Holy Spirit charged me with responsibility to pray and intercede for the Government mountain and the Media Mountain. There was a group of people following me but I did not look back to see who they were or how many were following. I kept my face like a flint on the mountain and did not allow anything to deter, or stop me from achieving my objective. It was a difficult task to push the baby carriage for three and a half years over every kind of terrain and obstacle but I never stopped, lost hope, or sight of the mountain. The first obstacle was a large field of wheat and tares about two feet high with no roads or a path through it.

Matthew 13:38
The field in the world; and the good seed are the sons of the kingdom and the tares are the sons of the evil one.

The baby carriage became the vessel to plow a path through the field so we could pass through. We were going through the world to make a way for giving birth to a new season. Some Christians and non-Christians try to discourage, hinder, and even try to stop your forward march toward your destiny. Sometimes God uses the things He puts in your hands as instruments to do the work or make a way. At another time a large male lion appeared in a dream in front of me and began fiercely roaring.

I had a gun in my hand and fired several shots at the lion, but they had no effect on the lion. The lion kept roaring and looking at me trying to make me afraid and run, but I stood my ground. Suddenly, the lion charged at me and I looked down and saw a long shaft(a shepherd' staff) and I bent down on my knees while looking at the lion.

I waited until he left the ground to leap on me and raised the shaft into the air while firmly placing the other end in the ground. The lion came down on the shaft and with its own weight pushing the shaft through its heart. This was a spiritual battle of doing warfare and God gave me the victory in a unique manner. The next obstacle I faced going toward the mountain was a fence stretching horizontal to the right and left as far as I could see. After surveying the fence, I decided it was too high to scale and it had no opening so we must make a detour. Sometimes the steps God has prepared for us are not in a straight line or the easiest way. He instructed Israel to take a lounger route for their good as seen in Exodus 13:17-18.

We simply must obey God and not question Him. I remember I was visiting my dad on a Sunday afternoon and I stayed a little too long. This caused me to be in a hurry to get to my church on time for Sunday night service. There was a shortcut that you had to cross the railroad tracks to take it.

The Holy Spirit spoke to me not to go that way, but I did not listen. There was a train sitting on the tracks and not moving. I waited and waited but it never moved. I finally turned my car around and went the way the Holy Spirit told me to go and I was a few minutes late getting to church.

Listen to the Holy Spirit even in the small things. We must be alert in our spiritual journey through life to discern the delays, detours, hindrances, and obstacles because sometimes they are for our own good to test or try us. The road signs could read patience, faith building, danger, slow down and rest.

Before we take action over a situation, we must determine if it is a trial from God, reaping from our sowing, or a hindrance from the devil.

The next obstacle was an old man who looked discouraged, sad, and despondent sitting on the bench of an old town. He was sitting with his back to the mountain and facing us. The old man tried to persuade us to take a break and visit an old rock church building with a Gothic style roof. This church looked like it belonged to the tenth or eleventh century. To me, this was a temptation of the enemy to look back to the past and get my eyes off the future. The old man did not care about the future or did not care what season he was in. He was content to stay in the old season and finish his course without changing. The path to the mountain went through the old town with cobblestone streets. It was very difficult to push the baby carriage through the cobblestone streets.

When the Holy Spirit has left the old season, we must move on or it will be difficult for us to stay, because we no longer have His anointing for the old season.

Jesus said his yoke was easy. We must keep this attitude and mindset that no matter how difficult the obstacle, it is easy to overcome with Jesus. We continued our journey and the mountain was getting larger as we drew closer and closer. The next event in the journey, we encounter another old man, however he was sitting on the bench that was parallel with our path to the mountain. This old man was excited, happy, and eager to help us and give us advice. This old man was completely opposite of the first old man at the entrance of the old city. I believe this represented the older generation who are willing to point the way to the future realm and season of God. He was an encourager to the new generation and was still willing to work for God to point out the direction to the next move of God.

We finally arrived at the base of the mountain and it was covered with underbrush and briars without a path or roads. This was the most physical part of the journey. We had to weave our way through the briar and underbrush. I remembered the story of the rabbit saying to the wolf, do not throw me into the briar patch but it was exactly where he wanted to go. We should desire the trials because this is where we grow in patience, faith, and perfection (James 1:3-4).

Jesus took His disciples through many difficult situations and they complained yet, they learned and grew in grace and knowledge of God. The next event was a tunnel that went through part of the mountain. This was the most frightening part of the journey. The tunnel was dark and full of evil spirits. We heard all kinds of blood curdling yells, sounds and screams. I told everyone to stay close to each other and have contact with each other. All kinds of demonic images appeared over our heads and at each side of us. Voices would laugh, mock, and say evil things to us to try to bring fear and stop our journey, but I encouraged everyone to keep their focus on the other end of the tunnel.

Psalms 30:5
For his anger endures but a moment; his favor is for life: weeping may endure for a night, but joy comes in the morning.

When we stay the course through the darkness of night there is always a joy and thrill of victory. We went through a great season of warfare at our church with everyone warring for their purposes to be fully pleasing to God. I had a dream with my back being covered with layers of flies. After the dream, I had an actual attack on my body. The weight was so heavy that I could barely walk. I literally had to crawl up the steps in our house. The Holy Spirit spoke to me that I was carrying the sins and burdens of others and I had to stand in the gap and intercede for them. The burdens had me lying on my face praying identification repentance prayers and waring for a week before the breakthrough came.

Back to the dream. We finally arrived at the top of the mountain. The top of the mountain had been leveled and there was an outdoor singing going on. The sound was terrible. There were all kinds of musical instruments but no one was in tune, the same beat or the same key. It sounded like an orchestra warming up with their instruments before a concert. Terrible! Just noise. My wife Phyllis and I started making a sound with our mouth, hands and feet. All the musicians stopped and picked up our beat and sounds and started playing the new sound and the new beat, tune, and key in unity. The new sound was beautiful and powerful. Like always, there were some who did not want to change and they rushed on Phyllis and pushed her to edge of the mountain. The Holy Spirit lifted her up and she floated to safety. Luke 4:28-30, Jesus was protected and led to victory by the Holy Spirit when the crowd tried to push Him over the cliff because they did not like what He said.

Part Two – Releasing a New Anointing.

The Holy Spirit spoke to me to go to Israel to Mount Zion to release the new sound and end time anointing of the Holy Spirit.

Isaiah 2:1-3

The word that Isaiah the son of Amos saw concerning Judah and Jerusalem. Now it shall come to pass in the latter days that the mountain of the Lord's house shall be established on the top of the mountains, and shall be exalted above the hills; and all the nations shall flow to it. Many people shall come and say, come, let us go to the mountain of the lord, to the house of the God of Jacob; He will teach us His ways, and we shall walk in His paths. For out of Zion shall go forth the Law, and the word of the Lord from Jerusalem.

My wife Phyllis gave a prophetic word that God was releasing a new sound of unity in the heart of the body of Christ. When she released this prophecy, the old windmill began to squeak and make noises and started turning. There was absolutely no wind blowing. All was calm and still. Our guide told us that the windmill did not work. It was a sign of the beginning of the new sound of unity and the wind of the Holy Spirit blowing across the world. Does unity produce a sound? Yes, music, singing, worship teams, and congregational worship, preaching and teaching can be great however, when all of these can come into unity with the sound of the Holy Spirit it creates a powerful sound of His anointing, presence, and authority. This process has the potential to produce any kind of positive results in the natural realm. I was raised in a Pentecostal church and have experienced great anointing. However, this is a new anointing of the Holy Spirit. When we get into the unity of the Holy Spirit there is a new sound released and you can only hear it as you also get in unity with the sound. It is not heard in the natural realm but only heard in the spiritual realm. Music, singing, and ministry can be anointed, yet there is a new sound on the anointing already present that can only be heard as you get in unity of the Holy Spirit. This is hard to explain. I can be in the anointing of the Holy Spirit listening to others ministering under the anointing and I no longer hear them but I hear a new sound of the Holy Spirit.

Part Three – Example of Unity.

To have a clear, full understanding of the unity of the spirit, we must travel back in time to the beginning of creation by God. God created Adam's body from the dust of the earth and breathed into his body His breath and life, thus creating three parts: body, soul, and spirit. Adam's spirit was alive and filled with God's nature. He could also see God, walk, and talk with him. When Adam sinned, his spirit went to sleep and he could no longer see and talk to God face to face. God started His redemption process of restoring man back to a relationship with Him.

The word unity is only listed three times in the Bible. First one is in the Old Testament **(Psalms 133:1, behold, how good and how pleasant it is for brethren to dwell together in unity).** Hebrew definition of unity is alike and together. God started the nation of Jews and instructed them not to marry other races of people. They were alike in circumcision, keeping feasts, animal sacrifices, Shabbat and the Torah (Law) but not in the spirit.

Deuteronomy 6:4
Hear, O, Israel: the Lord our God, the Lord is One. This became the Shema of Israel.

At this period of time the Godhead is one God. Let's move forward in time to the New Testament. The Greek definition of unity is one or oneness. God separates the Godhead and sends His word in seed form to a virgin, Mary. The word became flesh and is called Jesus **(John 1:14)**. After Jesus was crucified, resurrected, and goes back to Heaven, He sits down on the throne at the right hand of God **(Hebrew 1:12)**. Then Jesus sends the Holy Spirit to replace Him on earth and the Holy Spirit dwells in our spirit. Now there are three working in Heaven and on earth to show us the way to achieve unity of the spirit. God the Father on the throne, Jesus the Son seated at His right hand and the Holy Spirit on the earth living on the inside of us, yet they are one. This is the pattern or example of unity. Jesus would only say and do what the Father said to say or do.

Ephesians 4:1-3 – verse 3 says, endeavoring to keep the unity of the spirit in the bond of peace. Verse 4 says, there is one body and one spirit just as you were called in one hope of your calling. Jesus prayed for us to be one as He is one with His Father. So we know this is God's will for us to be one (John 17:20-23). Unity has to be achieved in three areas of our lives to follow the example of the Godhead. All three (spirit, soul, and body) must be working as one but our spirit has to be in control like God is in control of a Godhead.

Part Four – Unity of Spirit, Soul, and Body.

I Thessalonians 5:23
May the God of peace Himself sanctify you completely; and may your whole spirit, soul, and body be preserved blameless at the coming of Jesus.

- *All three must be in unity.*

Philippines 2:2
Make my joy complete by being of the same mind, maintaining the same love, united in spirit, intent on one purpose.

Our spirit, soul, and body has to be in unity or we cannot achieve unity with others or with God. Our soul and body must be submitted under the rule of our spirit. Self (soul) has to die and our spirit must be in control of our life. Then, our spirit must be surrendered to the rule and leadership of the Holy Spirit. We are commanded to let the Holy Spirit rule our lives.

Galatians 5:16
Walk in the spirit and you will not fulfill the lust of the flesh.

Walk is written in the imperative mood and continuous tense which is defined as a command by God to do it and do it at every moment. It is common knowledge we have to live our everyday lives and commitment of school or any jobs in the natural realm. So, how can I walk continually in the spirit? Since we released the new sound and end time anointing of the Holy Spirit I had a new experience with Him. I felt this overshadowing of the Holy Spirit cover me and I received a new awareness of His presence. This is different than discernment or hearing the voice of the Holy Spirit speaking. Before, I would ponder and ask, how can I walk continually in the spirit and fulfill my duties and objectives of life. Now, we can continually walk in the spirit in our awareness of His presence while we walk simultaneously in the natural realm. We can have total knowledge of both realms at the same time without problems. Praise God!

After this spiritual experience with the Holy Spirit, I was driving on the interstate to another city making 70 mph and suddenly, I was aware of the spirit of intercession upon me to pray. I was weaving in and out of traffic praying in tongues, doing warfare while driving 70 mph for about an hour.

I knew what was happening on the road and in the spirit praying at the same time. I wasn't caught away in the spirit as it sometimes happens and can happen, but I was operating both in the physical world and in the spiritual world simultaneously being fully aware of what I was doing in both realms.

This seems impossible but all things are possible with God. This is part of the new anointing of the end time prophecy of the Holy Spirit that we released in Israel. Unity is God's plan and can only be accomplished by him.

- *All Three must be Blameless and Holy.*

Keeping our spirit, soul, and body holy and blameless is a requirement by God to walk in oneness with Him in this life and qualify us for living the eternal life with Him. If our body and our soul cannot come under the authority of our spirit, we are not holy and blameless. Our body can sin and our soul can sin. The Bible list the sins of the body and the sins of the soul. We cannot allow either body or soul to rebel and do what they want to do and remain holy and blameless. Rebellion is disunity.

Amos 3:3
Can two walk together unless they are agreed?

The Godhead walks in unity and we cannot walk in unity with the Godhead if our spirit, soul, and body is not in unity.

Part Five – Progressive Maturity.

The Holy Spirit spoke to me and gave me the process of maturing our spirit, soul, and body. This process of maturing can be a great and positive experience or an alarming factor in a negative way. Maturity of spirit, soul, and body in a positive way produces sons of light or sons of God. Maturity of spirit, soul, and body in a negative way produces sons of darkness or sons of Satan. It is our choice who becomes our master.

II Peter 3:18
But grow in grace and knowledge of our Lord and Savior Jesus Christ.

This process will produce maturity to be like Jesus. How can we represent Jesus and be His ambassadors if we do not know Him or understand His standards?

Our Body

Everything starts with the body which houses our spirit and soul. The Bible compares the body with a temple or tabernacle. The tabernacle of Heaven has three parts: the outer court, the inner court and the Holy of Holies. Our bodies have three parts and the Holy of Holies houses our spirit which is part of the DNA of God himself. The body was created first by God when he created Adam. God then blew his life into Adam and he became a living soul. Our body is the vehicle that carries our spirit and soul wherever they want to go, and will do whatever it wants to do. This is why the devil attacks the body with sickness, diseases, and infirmities, and tries to destroy and kill the body. He also tries to destroy the body with piercings, tattoos, cutting, drugs, alcohol, tobacco, sexual immorality, gay, lesbian, prostitution, pimps, sexual sins, rape, pleasures of the world, lazy, don't want to work, pray, read Bible, go to church, or pay tithes.

Galatians 5:17
For the flesh sets itself against the spirit, and the spirit against the flesh; for these are in opposition to one another, so that you may not do the things you please.

The body has five senses that allows either the light of God or the darkness of the devil into our body.

- *Eye Gate – Luke 11:33-36*

The eye is the lamp of the body that brings light to the darkness inside of us. The correct translation of the condition of the eye is single and evil. What does being single imply? It is not plural. So, light and darkness cannot come in and occupy you at the same time. Neither a mixture of black and white which produces gray or a lukewarm condition. The law of physics states no two objects can occupy the same place at the same time. Light and darkness cannot occupy the same place at the same time because this produces a double standard of lifestyle. At any moment or at any time, you can act and talk like God and then change and be like the devil but not at the same time. *You are either acting like God or you are acting like the devil. When your eye is evil, your body is full of darkness.*

Luke 11:35 says, take heed that the light in you is not darkness.

Take heed is written in the imperative mood and the present tense. This is a warning and a command from God at every moment not to allow darkness to enter our body through the eye. Reality is, we have the potential to have maturity in our spirit, soul, and body depending on what kind light we allow in us. The truth is, the larger amount of light or darkness we allow in will determine whether the spirit, soul, and body will mature and dominate or rule over the others. What do we see? What kind of movies, TV, books, or magazines are before our eyes? All sexual material, demonic material, horror material, or any other material that has a content of darkness should not be viewed or our eyes to focus on.

I was working a secular job before I went full time as a pastor. Working in a coal mines where there is total darkness. Each miner wears a light on his hard hat to provide light for him to see. A slight movement of your head can be detected by the beam of light your individual light projects. At the beginning of the work shift, workers wait as a group in an area with wooden benches to sit down and wait for the boss to do a check to see if everything is safe for work. Each worker sits side by side and talks or snacks while they wait.

One day I was sitting between two men and they were passing a nude magazine back and forth between them across me and talking dirty talk. I didn't move my head in any direction to look at the book. I knew it was a nude, dirty sex magazine by the way they were talking. Later that day, another worker told me he had planned the whole thing to see if I would look at the magazine. He wanted to see if I was really a minister. He thanked me for not looking at the magazine and he told me, he now respected me as a minister. If we allow darkness to enter our body, the darkness of the devil will rule us.

- ***The Ear Gate.***

Again, according to a scientific study the ear is the second most important sense of the five. Hearing produces ten percent to twenty percent retaining ability in the brain. We are to guard our ears and prevent the sound of the world from bringing darkness to our bodies. We are constantly bombarded by the flow of false sounds of darkness from the news media, TV, radio, teachers, family, and ministers. Here again, just like our eyes, our ears can receive darkness and light. The truth is light and a lie is darkness.

If we listen to more darkness than light of truth, then our body will mature over our spirit and dominate our spirit. So, who do we listen to? How do we know who is lying? The Bible says in John 10:3-5, 27, my sheep know my voice and a stranger they will not follow. God is still speaking today. Even a natural baby quickly learns the voice and sounds of its mother and father. A new convert of Jesus can quickly learn the voice of the Holy Spirit through prayer.

Mark 4:24
Take heed what you hear, with the same measure you use, it will be measured to you, and to you who hear, more will be given.

Take heed is written in the imperative mood in present tense which is a command from God at every moment not to listen to the devil and bring darkness into yourself. Close your ears to all the negative talk or it will overpower your positive attitude.
 When a seed is planted, it has the potential to produce much fruit and the condition it produces can be good or bad depending on the positive or negative seed.

Romans 10:17
So then faith come by hearing and hearing by the word of God.

The ear gate is critical for your faith. What you hear can produce faith or fear. Again, take heed what you hear.

Hebrews 5:11
Of whom we have much to say, and hard to be explained since you have become dull of hearing.

One cannot hear because their hearing has become dull. Dull is defined as slow of heart, sluggish, and lazy. It is from the root word defined as a bastard or illegitimate child. Our soul and body can become so much more mature than our spirit that our spirit becomes weak and indifferent to God even to the point we no longer are in a relationship with Him. Our eye gate and ear gate together can produce a negative mindset so strong it captures us in the realm of darkness of negativity. The false teaching of grace has produced a lawless spirit in people that they think they can do anything they want to and be OK with God. *This produces a tolerance for sin.*

They become bastards and will be judged accordingly. Synergism takes place when you see and hear something at the same time. Retain ability of what you see and hear jumps to about 90%. This implies a mindset can be developed in either a positive or negative way of life. **A positive mindset means God is in control. A negative mindset means Satan is in control.**

- *Touch Gate*

Touch is defined as to exert a modifying influence upon an object or upon oneself. Touch can be negative or positive.

I Corinthians 7:1
It is good for a man not to touch a woman. Yet Jesus touched people and healed them.

Touch can be from the body and be negative or touch can be from the spirit and be positive. We cannot invade someone else's private domain. This is illegal. According to biology, the skin covers the whole body and has receptors in the skin to send signals to the brain. The receptors determine the sensation of touch to determine what you feel. There is a saying "do whatever feels good or feels right," however this is a lie from hell.

Feelings are stimulated by both good and bad sources. God produces sources of light which bring true happiness and victory however, the devil produces sources of darkness which produces fake happiness and defeat.

Alcohol, drugs, sexual immorality, porno, gay, lesbian, rape, prostitution, pimps, fornication, same sex marriages, produce feelings of pleasure that will separate one from God.

Also, false religions and beliefs produce feelings of false peace, joy, and belonging. So, you cannot rely on doing whatever feels good if you want to please God.

Proverbs 12:15
The way of a fool is right in his own eyes, but a wise man listens to counsel.

We cannot walk through life with God making decisions based upon feelings instead of His will. Most all reports have different research and opinions of feelings and emotions yet, none seems to be able to give a concrete or accurate analysis about the workings of feelings and emotions. There is a true feeling of the anointing and presence of the Holy Spirit that we must learn or discern to be led by Him.

- *Summary of the Body.*

Why did God create the body first?

1. God created the body first then breathed into it His life and Spirit. The body became the temple for the kingdom of God to dwell in. The body is the part seen and the devil wants to destroy what is seen. He wants to make God's creation to look cursed.

2. The body is the vehicle to transport the presence of God to the world. It acts like the ark carrying the word, power of the anointing of the Holy Spirit and God's provision everywhere we go and to all that will receive it.

3. The body was created to protect the spirit and soul. This is why the devil tries to destroy the body with sickness, disease, drugs, and murder. Cain killed Abel because Abel pleased God.

4. God gave us His full armor to protect the body and to stand against the strategies of the devil **(Ephesians 6:11-18)**. Even though God's armor is a spiritual armor it will protect the body much better than natural armor. I was traveling in my car and suddenly the Holy Spirit asked me a question. What was the first piece of armor God instructed us to put on? Why did God deem the belt of truth so important to use it first? What was the first thing God did after Adam and Eve sinned? He covered their nakedness, exposing their sexual organs. Why do several translations of the Bible leave out the word loin when it is in the Greek text?

Ephesians 6:14
Stand ye therefore girting round the loins of you with truth.

The definition of loin is generative or procreative power. God is linking the reproductive sexual organs and truth together. Why?

God is telling and showing us the two reproductive abilities of the body.

The first is that sex organs produce seeds of life.
Hebrews 7:9-10, Levi was in the loins of Abraham.

The second is that truth also produces seeds of life.

The first piece of armor God instructed us to put on was the belt of Truth to cover our loins. Our reproductive organs should be covered by the belt of truth that will protect us from sexual immorality. Sexual sins are so damaging to the present and future destiny of humanity. Sexual immorality destroys homes, marriages, lives, creates disease, and effects society. God is against all sexual immorality.

Truth is a word and words are seeds and seeds contain reproductive life. We can produce either negative or positive results in others by the power of our tongues speaking words. We can impregnate others with words or seeds or life or death. We can lead others astray from the truth.

If we have false beliefs and mindsets, we can pro create others to have the same false beliefs of life.

MATTHEW 12:37
FOR BY YOUR WORDS YOU SHALL BE JUSTIFIED, AND BY YOUR WORDS, YOU SHALL BE CONDEMNED.

The breastplate covers our heart and keeps us in right standing with God. The gospel is on our feet to keep us walking in the steps, and the way God has already prepared for us. The shield of faith has gone before us to protect us from the fiery darts, lies, accusations, and evil places of the devil. The helmet protects our minds from evil thoughts and thinking.
The sword is our defense and our offensive weapon to destroy the enemy(a two edged sword divides and separates). Prayer protects our tongue from creating all kinds of negative situations and

giving place to the devil. Finally, intercession keeps us from praying our own thoughts but allows the Holy Spirit to pray for the perfect will of God.

The Book of James states the tongue is an unruly evil, full of deadly poison, defiles the whole body and causes your purpose to be set on fire and destroyed. The body is so important to us that God gave us His full armor to protect it. Since God's armor is so critical to us, He commands us to put it on. It is not an option; a soldier puts on his own protection. We must daily protect ourselves by putting on God's armor in prayer. Paul says we must fight, and we would not be wise to face each day without our Godly armor.

Our Spirit

I believe we live beneath our full potential of the biblical definition of who God created us to be. Consider these facts with me. What happened to Adam when God breathed His life into him? Who did Adam become? What is the breath of life from God? Was it God's productive seed to become like him? What does it mean when the Bible tells us we are the children and sons of God? What does it mean when the Bible declares, we shall be like Him? Jesus was the son of God and He inherited all things. We then become joint heirs with Him. What does this mean?

Are we more than just a man?

The problem we have is that we think too small. We do not think like God. We have a grasshopper mentality. Our spirit is the part of God that He breathed into the body of Adam.

Our spirits are just like God.

It is his DNA in us. God is spirit and we are spirit. God is eternal and we are eternal. However, He put our spirit in a physical body thus placing limitations on us. Adam had the mind of God, the power of God, and the authority of God. He named all the animals and could talk to them and they obeyed. When Adam sinned, our spirits became disconnected from God and our abilities of God went to sleep.

Jesus bought us from the devil. By dying on the cross and shedding His blood, Jesus restored us to God the Father. Now, we are in the last season of restoration of all things. We are in the season of back to the Garden. I believe this is the last step of the bride of Christ making herself ready. We must accept the reality that God is restoring us to the spiritual state of Adam.

I Corinthians 15:44-49, Jesus was the second Adam, if we inherited all things through Jesus, we inherited the status of the second Adam. Could this be part of the wedding garment of putting something old on?

Let's take a small look at this question. We think of new as doing something different or not done before, but it has two definitions. There are two Greek words translated into English language for new. The word "new" has two different definitions in the Greek language.

1 – that which is unaccustomed or unused. New as to form or quality.

2 – new in time, recent, recently came into existence, never existing before.

Mark 2:21 (this verse has both definitions of new)

No one sews a piece of unshrunk (new, not existing before) cloth on an old garment, unless the new (as to form or quality) piece pulls away from the old and the tear is made worse.

Jesus is the word of the old covenant and the new covenant. *If you take a totally new word and add the new word to the old word this will create a divide or separation.*

However, if you take a new word that is not actually new to build on the old word, this will not create a divide or separation. **Galatians 3:24** The Old Testament is our schoolmaster.

We take the New Testament and build on the Old Testament to make it a better covenant. Let's look at the old Adam before he sinned and the new Adam that Jesus redeemed.

II Corinthians 5:17

Therefore, if anyone is in Christ, he is a new(new by qualitative better) creation, old things have passed away, all things have become new(qualitative better).

Ephesians 4:24

And clothe yourself with a new nature created to be Godly, which expresses itself in the righteous and holiness that flow from the truth.

I believe God is telling us we are the same spirit but we are new because we are better than the old. God has taken the new Adam and made him a better creation. Let's look at the old Adam. He could only walk and talk with God when God appeared to Him. Now, God lives inside of man in his spirit and he can walk with and talk to God anytime he wants too. Wow! Praise the Lord! This is great. We have the potential to be the sons of God and sit with Jesus on the throne of God and rule the earth because we are not entangled with the world and in bondage.

The Bible refers to man as children and sons of God. What is the difference? Let's clarify the difference between being a baby, children, and sons of God that the Bible calls us. Everyone is a child of God because He gave us His seed of birth when He breathed life into Adam(Romans 8:15-17). We are the children of God and joint heirs of Christ if we accept Jesus as our Savior. Verse 14, list a potential of being a son of God to those who are led by the Holy Spirit. As already stated, God compares the natural body and the spiritual body for us to form a clear understanding of the complete man. In the natural man, we go through stages of growth (infancy, childhood, adolescence and adulthood).

The spiritual realm of growth is the same. We are born again and become a spiritual infant or babe in Christ even if we are one hundred years old. There are different stages of spiritual growth until we reach a full mature son like Jesus. We know the natural characteristics of a baby and they are the same in the spiritual realm of growth. A baby cannot do anything for itself. It is totally dependent on someone else to take care of it. Our spirits cannot fight any battles or be led by the Holy Spirit as long as our spirit remains an immature Christian.

Galatians 4:1
Now I say that the heir, as long as he is a child or baby does not differ at all from a slave, though he is master of all.

Ephesians 4:20 refers to the same thing.

Ephesians 4:20
Now to him who is able to do exceedingly abundantly above all we ask and think, according to the power that works in us.

Even though we are joints heirs with Jesus and have inherited all things with Him, as long as we are babies and immature, we are like slaves and in bondage to self, soul, body and to darkness. We cannot overcome anything that the devil throws at us although we have power and authority over him because we do not have the knowledge. Why is this? The Holy Spirit in us is chained and made a slave by the lack of knowledge, by the desires of our soul, bodies, and immaturity.

How do we reach the status *"sons of God?"* How do we qualify ourselves to change from the infant stage?

- *We must be Spiritually Mature.*

Becoming sons of God demands spiritual growth. We cannot be immature in our spirit or we will not know how to operate the Holy Spirit in us.

Ephesians 4:13-15, until we all attain to the unity of the faith, and of the knowledge of the son of God, to a mature man, to the measure of the fullness of Christ.

As a result, we are no longer to be children or infants, tossed here and there by waves, and carried about by every wind of doctrine, by the trickery of men, by craftiness in deceitful scheming: but speaking the truth and love, we are to grow up in all aspects unto Him, who is the head, Christ.

We have the potential to have His mind, think His thoughts and look through His eyes, so why remain an immature baby. We are to become like Jesus to qualify ourselves as sons of God.

- *We also must believe we can become a son of God.*

Matthew 13:58
And he did not many mighty works there because of their unbelief.

If Jesus couldn't do great works because of unbelief, we cannot do them either, because it is Him in us doing the work.

Galatians 4:6-7
And because you are sons of God sent forth the Spirit of His Son into your hearts, crying out, Abba Father! Therefore you are no longer a slave but a son and if a son, then a heir of God through Christ.

We must believe it is God's will and potential for us to mature into the son of God.

Mark 9:24
Immediately, the boy's father cried out, "I do believe: help my unbelief."

This scripture is a classic example of a condition of most people. We believe, yet we have unbelief and this condition will not produce a son of God. We believe in our spirit but doubt it in our souls.

- *We cannot have a religious spirit and become sons of God.*

Matthew 23:27-28
Woe to you, scribes and Pharisees, and hypocrites!: for ye are like whitewashed tombs, which indeed appear beautiful outwardly, but inside are full of dead man's bones and all uncleanliness. Even so you are also outwardly righteous to men, but inside you are full of hypocrisy and lawlessness.

James 1:26
If anyone thinks himself to be religious, and does not bridle his tongue but deceives his own heart this man's religion is worthless.

A religious spirit is a group of evil spirits (legalism, self-righteous, false holiness, criticism, religious pride, judgement of others by their appearance, and false humility) that inspire loyalty to religious concepts and practices, to hinder or oppose the truth or the anointing of the Holy Spirit. A religious spirit operates out of the soul of man instead of the Holy Spirit.

John 10:22-31, the religious Jews would not believe or accept Jesus when He told them He was the Son of God and the Father and I are one. They took up stones to stone Him. That same religious spirit is prevalent today to attack anyone who says they are the sons of God, yet God tells us we are sons of God so accept it. Do you believe man or God? So does this make everyone sons of God or does this mean those who qualify as You say?

- *We must believe in the Holy Spirit.*

Romans 8:14 For all who are being led by the spirit of God, these are the sons of God.

Who is empowering us to do the same work that Jesus did? The Holy Spirit in us. We cannot be led by the Holy Spirit, if we do not believe He is a gift of God for us. If He is not in us, how can He led us? How can we walk in the steps God has already prepared for us? Because we cannot see them without the Holy Spirit revealing them to us. Jesus is our pattern. Matthew 3:16-4:1. Before He entered into His ministry, He received the Holy Spirit and was led by the Holy Spirit into the wilderness. When He finished His work on earth, He sent the Holy Spirit to dwell in us.

- *We cannot believe in wrong doctrines.*

Believing the wrong doctrine leads you away from God and into darkness. Jesus is the word of God manifested in flesh. God spoke the word from His mouth and the word became Jesus in the flesh. (John 1:14) He is the truth.

If we reject the truth, we are rejecting Jesus. If we are rejecting Jesus, how can we be sons? Accepting wrong doctrines, such as hyper-grace, causes you to accept sin thus making you sin and compromising the truth, thus disqualifying you as a son of God.

Example: I Corinthians 5:6-7 – A little leaven leavens the whole lump.

Romans 8:8-13 thus, these who identified with this old natural flesh cannot please God. Verse 12 so then, brothers, we don't owe a thing to our old nature that would require us to live according to our old nature. For, if you live according to your old nature you will certainly die: but if by the spirit, you keep putting to death the practice of the body, you will live.

John 7:16
Jesus answered them and said, my doctrine (teaching) is not mine, but His who sent me.

If our doctrine or teaching is not from God, but from our own ideas, imagination, thinking, theories, views, or understanding, we cannot be His son. Jesus only did what he saw His Father do and only spoke what He heard His Father say **(John 5:19, 12:49)**. We must do the same if we are the true sons.

God only watches over His word to fulfill it. Truth is the original intent of God. Truth is the standard of God. You can push the truth to the extreme left(a liberal view)and step out into air without a foundation to stand on and fall or you can push the truth to the extreme right(a conservative view) and fall short in receiving all that the truth provides. Only what He says is covenant.

It is our responsibility to enter in a covenant with what He says and not what we think. We have His faith to believe what He says however, we must use our faith to believe what we say.

Big difference. How can we be one with God and believe our own doctrine?

- *We must separate ourselves from the World.*

II Corinthians 6:17-18
Come out from among them and be separate says the Lord. Do not teach what is unclean, and I will receive you. I will be a Father to you, and you shall be my sons and daughters, says the Lord Almighty.

Separate is defined as divide, mark off by boundaries. We must establish boundaries and not cross them. Holy Spirit spoke to me that separate means to separate to and from.

We must separate ourselves to God and separate ourselves from the world. We must the two edged sword of Spirit in between us and the world.

Acts 17:26
From one man, He made every nation of men to settle upon all the face of the earth, after He determined fixed times and boundaries of their habitations.

Proverbs 13:9
He who guards his mouth preserves his life. Definition of guard is to protect, to keep. This is setting a boundary over your mouth.

Exodus 32:19-29. After Moses received the commandments from God, he came down from Mount Sinai and found the people dancing, wild sounds, all kinds of actions and worshiping idols. Moses divided the people into those that were on God's side and the rest were destroyed. He ordered the people to consecrate yourselves to God.

As I have previously said, God and His Kingdom of light and Satan and his kingdom darkness cannot operate in you at the same time. So, we must set boundaries from the devil and the world to keep us pure and holy.. To receive the spiritual status of a son of God, we must come out of the world and live the lifestyle that God requires. There cannot be any compromise with the world and be a son of God. When you divide something, there is no more mingling. We cannot mix Godlessness and worldliness and please God.

Revelations 3:15
Jesus said, I know your works and you are neither cold or hot. I wish you were cold or hot. So because you are lukewarm, I will vomit you out of my mouth.

- *We must accept chastening from God.*

Hebrews 12:7-8
If ye endure chastening, God deals with you as sons; for what son is there whom the father chastens not? But if ye be without chastisement, whereof all are partakers, then all ye are bastards and not sons.

Definition of chastening denotes the training of a child by instruction, discipline and correction. When we are born again, we become a child of God and must receive chastening from God our father to develop into a son.

God loves us and has planned our lives to be good, successful, and prosperous, and has prepared Heaven for our final destination to live with Him so He does everything He can to help us get there.

- *We must be Peacemakers.*

Matthew 5:9
Blessed are the peacemakers for they shall be called sons of God.

Definition of peacemakers: The one who makes peace in others having first received the peace of God in his own heart; not simply one who makes peace between two parties. A baby cannot produce a child neither can a baby christian produce a son of God.

This is why Jesus could call the peacemaker a son of God.

God has plans for us to be restored to the original state of Adam. Jesus was the second Adam and walked in relationship with God as a son in the flesh, performed many signs, wonders, and miracles, defeated the devil, cast out demons, lived a holy lifestyle, obeyed and pleased God, was filled with the Holy Spirit, was spiritually motivated, and followed only the doctrine of God. He said we could do the same and greater works shall you do (John 14:12).

Jesus' spirit controlled His soul and body and we can do the same and have the same results. We can be the same Adam because we are joint heirs with Jesus. We can bring peace to others and restore them to a peaceful relationship with God.

Our Soul

Our soul is the third part of man God created. I believe the spirit and soul were linked together but when Adam sinned the spirit went to sleep and was cut off and separated from the soul and from God. The soul or self was activated and became the dominant controlling part of man.

Genesis 2:17
God said, the tree of knowledge of good and evil you shall not eat, for in the day you eat of it you shall surely die.

Genesis 3:5
The serpent said to Eve, "for God knows that in the day you eat of it your eyes will be open, and you will be like God, knowing good and evil."

Obeying Satan created a divided wall in Adam and Eve. This dividing wall separated their spirit from God, their spirit from the soul, and they came to the knowledge of good and evil. At that time a struggle began in them whether to obey God and do good or obey Satan and do evil. Three kingdoms were established in man. The kingdom of self, the kingdom of God, and the kingdom of Satan. Which one would rule or influence our life?

Thus, a war zone was created in man. Man was being led and dominated by his soul until Jesus reclaimed man's spirit thus, transferring the dominion of the soul to the dominion of the spirit. It has been a struggle and war for man. A majority of humanity is still living a soul dominated lifestyle because the soul is made up of our mind, will, and emotions of hate, jealously, bitterness, envy, strife, ego, sadness and selfishness, etc..

The emotions of the soul can fill all the manifestation of the fruit of the spirit without a true lifestyle of Jesus. Because the soul is not a part of God's spirit, it only produces a similarity of the fruit. Love, joy, and peace produced by the soul is not as powerful as love, joy, peace produced by the Holy Spirit in your spirit.

Love, joy, and peace from your soul is from your emotions while love, joy, and peace from your spirit is from the life of God.

Your soul is guided and influenced by your self-life and your spirit is guided by the Holy Spirit. Paul says there is a war going on between soul and spirit to see which one is the dominate one to direct your life. James tells us the tongue is connected to both your soul and your spirit and it can only be connected to one at a time, therefore when our tongue is connected to our soul (influenced by Satan and darkness) we create acts of flesh and death that cannot please God. When our tongue is connected to our spirit (influenced by God) we produced His life and light. Again, according to science two objects cannot occupy the same space at the same time. Since diseases can be produced from our body, spirit, and soul, we must discern and recognize the source and make the right decision between good and evil.

I believe since we can operate as the second Adam, we have a greater ability to know right from wrong.

Our spirits host the Holy Spirit in the Kingdom of God, we have the power and authority to do great exploits because God is in us. God created our spirits to rule and dominate our body and soul. Only as we allow this can there be unity of man. So, we can never achieve unity of the spirit unless self-dies and we bring our soul, and body under the leadership of the Holy Spirit in our spirit, and develop spiritual maturity so our spirits can rule our soul and body.

CHAPTER 7

MAKE LIFE AN ADVENTURE

There are a lot of negative expressions about the practical experiences of life.

- *Life is full of hard knocks.*
- *I can't do it.*
- *Life is full of gloom, despair, and agony.*
- *Life has passed me by.*
- *Whatever will be, will be.*

There are also a lot of positive expressions about the practical experiences of life.

- *Life is ten percent what happens to you and ninety percent how you react to it.* **-Chuck Swindoll**
- *Only I can change my life. No one can do it for me.* **-Carol Burnett**
- *Failure will never overtake me if my determination to succeed is strong enough.* **– Og Mandino**
- *I can do all things through Christ.*

The Bible says we are more than conquerors, have dominion over our sphere of influence, and rule and reign with Jesus. Everyone has their ups and downs as they travel down life's path on their way to their eternal destiny. Why then do some get back up and go on and some never seem to arise from their adversity?

My wife and I have counseled people who have lost their hope and cannot pull themselves out of darkness to see the light. I have visited and talked to the homeless in different places and they all seem to no longer care.

While street witnessing in Washington D.C., I talked to a homeless street man and I was shocked to hear what he said. I told him that I could help him but he told me that he did not want my help. He said he had given up on life. He could no longer face reality. He would rather sleep on the streets, take hand-outs, have no possessions, and eat free meals at the shelters than take responsibility for anything.

Their minds have totally been captivated by the negative realm of impossibilities. Ultimately, they care about no one but themselves and do not contribute anything to society or other people. It is sad to see them with such low self-esteem and wasting their gifts, talents, potential, and purpose.

Help and deliverance is only one thought away.

We are only one thought away from living in the negative realm of defeat and entering the positive realm of victory.

One thought of thinking "I can" instead of I can't will change your life. You are only one thought away from who you are to whom you can be.

The Secret Life of Walter Mitty is the only short story I remember from High School. Walter Mitty could be anyone he wanted to be in a moment of time, in his imagination. Remove the pattern of thinking from the fantasy world to the world of reality by changing our thoughts from the negative thought of I dread or I can't to the positive of I do not dread because I can do it. Living in a fantasy world, like Walter, is optional, however, you can apply the same principles of one thought away to be positive instead of being negative.

Looking through the eyes of the Holy Spirit will always produce a positive attitude. Looking through the eyes of the soul will produce a negative attitude.

Joy is the fruit of the spirit while sadness is an emotion of the soul.

We have talked about assimilation of the truth to become like Christ. If we can get this seed of truth of "I can" into our spirits, then we can see the transformation process before our eyes. The Holy Spirit spoke to me a word that will change everyone's outlook on life. ADVENTURE!!! He said to make everything you do an adventure. Who doesn't like an adventure? You do not have to take an exotic trip or watch movies to have an adventurous life.

You should think, see and expect everything to be an adventure instead of being, unexcited and routine. Expect it in your everyday living in the workplace, at school, in your marriage, family, and your church.

Remember the famous quote from Ralph Waldo Emerson, "Nothing great was ever achieved without enthusiasm."

Making everything an adventure is quite simple. We only need to make a minor adjustment to our thinking. Think on it for thirty days and you have developed a mindset. A mindset starts a pattern to be formed and soon your adventure will become a routine without thinking about it.

Psalms 16:11
You will show me the path of life; in your presence is fullness of joy; at your right hand are pleasures forevermore.

David is confessing God will show him how to walk through life's journey in His presence which provides fullness of joy and pleasure. Notice the requirement for this to happen. First, you have to be seated at the right hand of God through Jesus Christ and be in His presence of His thoughts that of all things are possible.

This potential has already been provided for us through Jesus and the Holy Spirit. This is not a separate walk or path from your routine work or school schedule. As you walk down this path there are delightful pleasures and joy, so make a choice to make it an adventure instead of a dread. The only difference is looking through the Holy Spirit's eyes instead of the eyes of your soul.

When you develop this pattern, you can walk in the awareness of this spiritual dimension and still perform your daily duties. Walking in the spirit is an awareness of God's presence in your spirit and doesn't take away from your focus to perform all your work and school duties in excellence. This will not distract you from doing your normal obligations but it will create an adventurous attitude of looking for someone or something to show your kindness or adventurous appreciation and will bring them and you pleasures in life.

Exodus 12:11, God tells Israel to get ready to leave Egypt and put a belt on your waist, your sandals on your feet, your staff in your hand, and eat your Passover meal in haste and be ready to go. Wow!! You talk about an adventure. They have never been anywhere because they were in bondage for four hundred and thirty years. They did not know where they were going, how to get there, or what they were going to eat or drink. I believe they were excited. However, like everyone else, they lost their excitement by doing the same routine and eating the same old thing day after day. They lost their adventurous thinking of what will happen tomorrow. Instead, they had their old thinking of dreading tomorrow.

We must enter each day with a mindset of adventure of what God has planned while doing and fulfilling our obligations of living and existing.

Jesus said to love our neighbors as ourselves. So, allow Him to show or tell us how to love our neighbor every new day. This is adventurous. When the Holy Spirit spoke to me "to make everything we do an adventure," He also give me the scripture reference.

Matthew 13:44
The Kingdom of Heaven is like a treasure hidden in the field, which a man found and hid, and from joy over it, he goes and sells all that he has and buys the field.

To me, this is an overwhelming example of an adventure. Let's define each word on the next page:

1. **Like** is defined as resembling, same as, similar, a comparison. Kingdom of Heaven is like. Like what? This verse is comparing what Jesus is saying to how the kingdom works. He uses a hidden treasure. We can insert a marriage, dating, working to become one, having children, working jobs, buying homes and food, becoming a son of God like Jesus, and anything we do as a hidden treasure.

2. **Treasure** is defined as a deposit, wealth.

3. **Hidden** is defined as concealed, and is in the passive voice, perfect tense which is an action taken in the past but has existing results. The field was acted upon by God in the past when He placed the treasure there before the foundation of the world and it waits on us to find it.

4. **Field** is defined as a piece of ground, a cultivated field. Our body is full of dirt being made by God from the dust of the earth.

5. **Hide** is defined as not revealed, keep secret.

6. **Joy** is defined as cheerfulness, gladness, to rejoice.

7. **Sells** is defined as to sell.

8. **Buy** is defined as take possession, purchase, redeem. What is God saying? What is God telling us?

A. The Kingdom of Heaven is like an adventure.

B. The treasure is our purpose, gift, calling from God placed in us in times past before the world was formed.

II Corinthians 4:7
But we have this treasure in earthen vessels that the excellence of the power may be of God and not us.

C. The treasure is hidden inside of our body and our spirit. Accepting Christ as our personal savior or being born again reveals the Kingdom of God lying dormant or asleep on the inside of us. This process activates and restores our spiritual relationship to God.

D. We are the field the treasure is hidden in. Because of Adam's sin, our spirit has been hidden on the inside of us until we find it by accepting Jesus. The field is our spiritual house made from God and living in our bodies (made from dirt).

E. What does it mean to find a treasure hidden and you find it, yet you hide it again? Could it be when you are born again, you are considered a baby Christian and do not produce much light? As long as you are a baby, you are a heir, yet, you are a slave. Your purpose to rule and reign is hidden in your immaturity.

F. Joy is the excitement, happiness, and cheerfulness experienced when Jesus comes into your heart. Because of this joy, you can make any kind of sacrifice needed to make an adventure.

G. Willing to sell all you have to purchase the whole field and not just the treasure. This requires you to die to self, die to the world, switch allegiance from the devil to God, changing your lifestyle, and demeanor. You become willing to do whatever it takes to not only find and buy the treasure, but to fully experience and enjoy the fullness of the treasure.

H. You buy your whole life, your past and you future, whatever the cost. You take ownership of your whole being (spirit, soul, and body) from the devil and give it all to God by becoming His servant and child. This requires placing a value on your life. What you do not place a high value on, you will not keep or complete this journey.

Also, you must prioritize your actions and behavior to keep possession at whatever the cost. Your purpose is at stake, your destiny is at stake, so what is it worth to you? We may have a daily routine and life may not be easy, however, we must make everyday an adventure for God.

In 1960, my dad and I attended an old outside camp meeting. For lunch, they served hamburgers and you went through a line to buy your own food. Dad ordered two hamburgers and two fries and two drinks. As he neared the end of the line, he realized he never eats but one burger and fry. Standing near the end of the line was an older man and dad asked him if he would like some food. The man said, yes.

We sat down and talked to him. He told us about his ministry and it broke my heart. He was a minister, he had no vehicle, no possession, no home, no family, and no income. All he had was a small suitcase. He wasn't complaining, discouraged, gloomy or sad but excited to be used by God. He totally depended on God. The Holy Spirit would tell him where to go and he would start walking. People would give him a ride and buy him food. Yet, the man was so happy and full of joy to be alive and serving God. This is one of the greatest examples of making everything you do an adventure.

II Corinthians 2:14-17
Thanks be to God who always leads us in triumph in Christ, fragrance of His knowledge in every place.

Definition of triumph is, leads us to victory. Use the thrill of victory to make everything we do an adventure. This scripture implies a Roman general leading the defeated king in a triumphant march into the city with his crown, celebrating, cheering, and thrilled. This is a picture of what God wants us to have as we enter each new day. The second part of the scripture tells us we release a fragrance or an odor to those we come in contact with. If we show or display a life of gloom and despair and negative outlooks we release a stinking, revolting fragrance of dead works, works of the flesh. However, if we show or display the life of adventure of joy and victories, we release a fragrance of life in the spirit. This aroma will create a desire in someone to have what we have.

I was in sports and I loved the ABC sports lead in commercials, the thrill of victory and agony of defeat. This lead in became a part of my mindset and I used it to motivate me to win and be victorious over every obstacle of the devil in pulling down strongholds. This motivated my wife and me to travel to seventy nine countries tearing down strongholds over them.

To make everything I do, an adventure is my short term goal for each new day of my life and my long term goal of doing it the rest of my life.

CHAPTER 8

CONCLUSION

A season is a design from God and is for man's benefit, success, and part of our inheritance. A spiritual season has a set time, yet, we do not know the length of the season. Seasons can last a minute, an hour, a day, a month, or years. It is our responsibility to find out.

The main seasons are corporate seasons for everyone, yet, sometimes, there are personal seasons within a corporate season. Sometimes personal time is given from God to individuals to be processed. There are also personal seasons of trials and reaping to awaken us to see our shortcomings, weakness and strengths.

The length of a personal season depends on us and our submission to be processed, changed and matured into whom God has designed us to be. God uses seasons to develop us into sons of God to become fully like Jesus. Going through seasons with a casual attitude of not fully understanding each cycle will not produce the full result God has planned. Some of the cycles listed in this book demanded a full explanation while others didn't.

There are two distinct factors why people are against the changes of a new season.

1. Familiarity – example Israel. Israel prayed to get out of bondage and God delivered them, yet, they complained and argued about their new season of deliverance.

2. Looking back instead of looking forward. Going forward demands change and weakening old patterns and mindsets. This is not easy unless you apply the principles of a new cycle written in this book.

Proverbs 4: 20-22
My son, give attention to my words; Incline your ears to my sayings. Do not let them depart from your eyes; Keep them in the midst of your heart; For they are life to those who find them, and health(medicine) to all their flesh.

Instructions from God are comparable to a natural doctor's prescription both contain medicine to help your problem. Failure to listen to either of them will not produce healing results.

1 Thessalonians 5:23
May the God of peace make you completely holy, may your entire spirit, soul, and body be kept blameless for the coming of our Lord Jesus Christ.

The word sanctify is defined as holy, to withdraw from fellowship with the world and from selfishness by first having fellowship with God and toward God. I pray for everyone reading this book to hear and help fulfill Jesus' last prayer for us to be one with God and each other. Before this can happen, we must be one with ourselves in our spirit, soul, and body. Paul says there is a war going on in us between flesh and spirit. Until we stop this war and allow our spirit to be in control of our lives there cannot be peace with ourselves, with others, or with God. We can do this because of the pattern of Jesus, the power of the Holy Spirit and the mindset that all things are possible to those who believe.

I attended a soul winning conference for a week of intensified training in every aspect of soul winning. We had teaching and training in the morning and in the evenings, we went out in the community and applied what we had learned.

One day we visited the prison, which was prearranged. The men were led into an area called, the bullpen, and we lined up in front of the prison bars. The prisoners were in the back of the cell and they could both come forward and stand in front of the one they selected or not come forward.

We were trained to have an opening dialogue and what to say or not to say. As I was walking in front of the cell, The Holy Spirit told me not to use the normal opening dialog. This was in July and it was hot and the prison was hot and the prisoners only had on shorts.

A tall skinny man walked up to me and he had tattoos all over his body. He was very skinny and his hair was long and dirty. His teeth were decayed and he looked so sad and despondent.

I greeted him with, I love you and Jesus loves you. This stunned him. Later, I found out why. I allowed the Holy Spirit to speak through me to give him words of comfort and release and I was able to lead him to the Lord. His countenance changed, he cried, he felt the Spirit of the Lord and he told me he would start changing his life. Praise God.

We were trained and instructed to turn in names and results of everything we did each day. I turned in my report to the instructor and he questioned me about the prisoner. He said he was making sure I had the right prisoner because the school had been trying for two years to get him to pray. This was overwhelming joy for me. Make each day an adventure to always be ready to help someone in need or give a positive word. Be a sweet smelling fragrance to others by giving them the truth.

Everyone has a choice to dread each new day or to make each new day an adventure. Jesus choose to make his crucifixion an adventure even through all the suffering he endured.

Hebrews 12:2-3
Fixing our eyes on Jesus, the author and finisher of our faith, who for the joy that was set before Him endured the cross, despising the shame and has sat down at the right hand at the throne of God. For consider Him who has endured such hostility by sinners against Himself, so that you may not grow weary, lose heart, and discouraged in your souls.

Galatians 6:9
And let us not grow weary while doing good, for in due season we shall reap if we do not lose heart.

Jesus is our pattern to follow. Jesus operated 100% out of His spirit and 0% from His soul. Adam operated 100% from his spirit for a while but, later, switched to his soul. Adam didn't keep his soul blameless and was judged by God and lost his inheritance including his relationship with God and living in the Garden of Eden. Can this happen to us today? Yes. We must keep all three parts of man blameless. I Thessalonians 5:23 says keep the whole spirit, soul, and body blameless. Whole is defined as having all the parts sound and perfect. It expresses man before the fall. Look for the different seasons from God, apply the cycles of the seasons and you will be successful in life and pleasing to God. Missing a cycle is like missing part of a school year in the natural realm, it is very difficult to catch up with all the information and experience you miss. I pray that you will achieve the full stature of Jesus Christ also, that you remember, do not lose heart or become weary but to make life an adventure.

My Prayer For You

Heavenly Father, You are the creator of the universe and both the natural season and the spiritual season. Forgive me if I have failed to follow the seasons during my life because of either ignorance or being passive to Your will. Help me to enter the current season and to catch up on what I have missed. I want to be a participator in this last season and not a bystander. I want to mature and be like Jesus, fulfill my purpose, and reach my destiny. Thank you for hearing me and answering me.

Amen.

Other Books by Pastor Kenneth Sturgill

Leaving and Entering
Your Future is Now
Come Up Higher
Rejection Revealed

Contact
ksturgill@comcast.net

Made in the USA
Middletown, DE
08 October 2024